SpringerBriefs in Law

More information about this series at http://www.springer.com/series/10164

Rosanna Masiola · Renato Tomei

Law, Language and Translation

From Concepts to Conflicts

Springer

Rosanna Masiola
Social and Human Sciences Department
International University 'Stranieri' of Perugia
Perugia
Italy

Renato Tomei
Social and Human Sciences Department
International University 'Stranieri' of Perugia
Perugia
Italy

ISSN 2192-855X ISSN 2192-8568 (electronic)
SpringerBriefs in Law
ISBN 978-3-319-14270-8 ISBN 978-3-319-14271-5 (eBook)
DOI 10.1007/978-3-319-14271-5

Library of Congress Control Number: 2015932075

Springer Cham Heidelberg New York Dordrecht London

Printed on acid-free paper

Springer International Publishing AG Switzerland is part of Springer Science+Business Media (www.springer.com)

Language is the highest manifestation
of social unity in the history of mankind,
and it is the inherent right of each group
of people to use its language without
restriction.

Nelson Mandela

Preface

The present study reflects the combined experience of the authors as teachers and translators in the fertile area of cross-cultural studies of law and international communication. It is based on postgraduate courses, the *LawLab: Communicating Legal English* (2013) and doctoral seminars held at the Department of Human and Social Sciences, International University 'Stranieri' of Perugia.

Debates with students on aspects of law and communication feature topics and issues for which the authors can only provide partial solutions, and we are well aware that this field of research raises more questions than possible answers. Sometimes there are many answers, but they are not always adequate. Diachronic changes in culture, law and language are an important dynamic factor and, more often than not, a bilingual or multilingual dictionary cannot provide quick solutions. On the other hand, the field of legal translation has increasingly relied on communication from and into English. Long before the digital era and globalization, the field of insurance transactions in English served as a model for insurance companies in the Western world. Lloyd's 'Institute and Cargo Clauses' (ICC) was the plague of the translator: was it 'hook damage' or 'pilferage' when bags of coffee were damaged? And what was an adequate Italian equivalent? The ICC is currently used all over the world to settle claims, a fact that often necessitates substantial pragmatic interpretation.

Students of language and law always strive to find 'the perfect' word in legal translation. Theories of interpretation may offer sophisticated models to refer to when discussing philosophy of law and language: yet the hands-on work of translating the right word and concept into another tongue is not always the same thing. Chapter 2 of the survey illustrates different approaches to the theory of language and law.

The task seems daunting when dealing with language and law, and even more so with the English and Italian languages and their respective legal systems. Signposts, however, may be of help. There are cultural filters, lexical constraints and there are, moreover, two different legal systems, as analyzed in the third chapter. Even in what appears to be a well-known and widespread criminal offense, there are shifts in register and variations in terms within the English language. A thematic approach has, therefore, been adopted to illustrate diachronic and diatopic variation in the same offense, starting from the first words recorded in dictionaries, e.g. 'abduction' and '*abigeato*.' 'Abduction,' as in Charles Sanders Peirce's system of signs and logic is not the same as 'abduction' used in the sense of 'cattle stealing.' The topic of 'cattle stealing' is approached through comparative topics in the fourth chapter of the research, in light of the fact that food supply is a major issue for survival. The link between this theme and the wars it has caused across borders introduces the conclusive chapter of the study. The last section focuses on international treaties in translation and includes colonial, postcolonial and global case studies. It starts with the conquest of the 'New World,' the Indian wars and the Mexico-American wars (caused by cattle raiding), and then moves on to more recent events.

The LawLab Unit, with its outstanding students, was a testing ground for exploring the different potentials in the context of communicating and translating legal English, and pinpointing dynamics in cross-cultural communication. Exploring the words of the law in the different systems opened uncharted (albeit not unchartered) territory where literature, philosophy, history and ideology could be recomposed and united in a multidisciplinary, cross-cultural and thematic approach to legal language. This is one small, perhaps clumsy step; as such, if we stumble or fall, such lapses are entirely our responsibility. If punishment follows crime, this entry from the Jamaican English Dictionary epitomizes the ambiguity of the word 'law' intended as 'punishment.'

If a kech yu, a giv yu a laa fom-fom tide

(If I catch you today I'll give you a (law) sound thrashing)

(Dictionary of Jamaican English: law)

Acknowledgments

This survey was written as a first response to Prof. Pietro Perlingieri's challenge to address questions of translation. Giovanni Paciullo, Rector of the International University 'Stranieri' of Perugia, has been an enthusiastic supporter of our initiatives in the field of legal science and translation.

Discussions broadened the cultural perspective, extending it toward classical philosophy, hermeneutics and the scholarly tradition of the Neapolitan 'scuola crociana.' The domain of law and language and the current scenario seem to point to a threatening clash of languages and cultures, from food theft to international treaties and crossing over to legal and geographical areas 'where angels fear to tread.' We took up the challenge of breaking down barriers, and assume full responsibility for the success or failure of this venture.

Last, but not least, we would like to thank the Springer team for their constant assistance and professional support, especially Anke Seyfried for answering emails when normally people are away on holidays. Special thanks also to Matt Fentem for his expertise and reliability in proofreading, and the Chennai team in India with Alexander N.S.R, for all their patience in handling production.

Perugia, London, December 2014

Acknowledgments

This survey was written as a first response to Prof. Flavio Fe[illegible] address questions of translation. Giovanni Pascuillo, R[illegible] University "Sapienza" of Rome, has been an enthusiastic [illegible] s in the field of legal science and translation. [illegible]

Contents

1	**Introduction**	1
	References	4
2	**Theoretical Concepts**	5
	2.1 Preliminary Observations	5
	2.2 Introductory Topics: From Theory to Theme	6
	2.3 Concepts and Definitions	7
	2.4 Materials and Methods	8
	2.5 A Comparative Thematic Approach	10
	2.6 Conceptual Meaning: Indeterminacy and 'Subsumption'	11
	2.7 Validity in Interpretation and Hermeneutics	13
	References	16
3	**Definitions and Applications**	19
	3.1 Functions and Contexts	19
	3.2 Legal Discourse: 'Obstruction of Justice'	20
	3.3 Lexicography and Translation	21
	3.4 Conceptual Lexicon: Liberty, Crime and Felony	23
	3.5 Hierarchy in Meaning: 'Rule'	26
	3.6 International Legal English	27
	3.7 Plain English, Law and Literature	28
	References	33
4	**A Global Crime and World Hunger**	35
	4.1 Cattle Stealing: Europe and the Greek Myth	35
	4.2 Legends of the Wild West	36
	4.3 South of the Border: More Languages, More Laws	37
	4.3.1 Messing with Texas: Rustling and Ranching	39
	4.4 Duffing Down-Under: Australia and New Zealand	40

4.5 Africa and Jamaica: Blood Compensation and Machetes 43
4.6 India: Holy Cows 45
References. 46

5 Conflicts and Clashes 47
5.1 Concepts and Crimes 47
5.2 'Possessions' and Colonial Conquest. 49
5.3 Clashes of Cultures: Signs, Symbols, Symptoms. 50
5.4 Ethnic Cleansing: Aborigines and the Law. 52
5.5 Defining 'Genocide' and 'Democracy' in Africa. 55
5.6 Translation: Ethics, Culture and Ideology 57
5.7 Transactions and Diplomacy: China and Hong Kong 59
5.8 Europe and Beyond: No Translation, No War 63
5.8.1 Germany and Austria: The Congress of Vienna 65
5.8.2 First World War Manifesto 66
5.9 Conflict Areas: Geographic Boundaries 68
References. 71

6 Manipulating Treaties 73
6.1 Intranational Treaties: Maori and New Zealand. 73
6.2 The Trail of Broken Treaties and North-American Indians 77
6.3 Conflicting Interpretations: East Africa 85
6.4 Concluding Remarks. 92
References. 93

Abbreviations

BLD	*Black's Law Dictionary* (1996) USA
CED	*Collin's English Dictionary* (2000) UK
DDC	*Doucet's Dictionnaire du Droit Criminel* (2014) FR
DEL	*Legal English. Dizionario Inglese Italiano* (2009) Italy
DES	*Dictionary of English and Spanish* (1998) (Mexico-US)
DII	*Dizionario Inglese Italiano Inglese* (2001) Italy
DIL	*Dizionario di inglese legale applicato* (2012) Italy
ETIL	*English–Italian Law Dictionary* (2011) Italy
F DG	F. de Franchis (1984) *Dizionario Giuridico—Law Dictionary*
JED	*Jamaican English Dictionary* (2002) West Indies
OLD	*Osborn's Concise Law Dictionary* (2013) UK
OXDL	*Oxford Dictionary of Law* (2013) UK
PEG	*Piccola Enciclopedia Giuridica* (1959) Italy
WLCD	*West's Law and Commercial Dictionary* (1988) Italy

See also full references and online sitography.

Chapter 1
Introduction

This study tackles the problem of communication and the practice of translation, which constantly interfaces with theoretical issues in interpretation and conceptualization arising from the philosophy of law and language. As noted by some authors (Morris 1995; Joseph 1995), no other discipline is so indebted to the philosophical and theoretical debate. It is, however, utterly devoid of power if there is no practical counterpart and meaning is not communicated, negotiated, and translated. Translation can be done on an intra-linguistic, inter-linguistic or inter-semiotic level (Jakobson 1966). Recent multi-modal analysis applied to short video sequences highlighting legal communicative practices may also be a useful tool when audiovisual translation is needed (Taylor 1998).

The globalization of media, the resonance of crime and punishment, law and order, the winds of war and terrorism have now made it mandatory to acquire more refined tools for instant translation. In breaking news, the media must cope with different languages and idioms in order to communicate 'crimes and punishment.' Meaning and communication of meaning is the key issue here (Nelken 1996; Van Hoecke 2002; Beke 2014), along with its enactment across different cultures, languages and legal systems (Azar 2007).

The no-longer hegemonic power of the Western world's legal systems inevitably meet with traditions where identity, values, beliefs and environment are interwoven and differ from culture to culture (Katan 1999). Islamic law and the evolving Chinese world are just two examples. There are also the mixed traditions of India and the constitutional laws of African states. In most cases, the legal system is bilingual or multilingual, usually interfacing with English (Tiersma 2012; Morris 1995; Cao 2007).

Gandhi and Mandela spread their ideas and acquired prominence through the medium of English. They spoke English in addition to their native tongues, as both India and South Africa feature an incredible number of languages and linguistic communities. Mohandas Granchand Gandhi studied law at University College in London (UCL), and Nelson Rolihlahla Mandela studied law at the University of Witwatersrand, and they both practiced as lawyers in South Africa. Their mother

R. Masiola and R. Tomei, *Law, Language and Translation*,
SpringerBriefs in Law, DOI 10.1007/978-3-319-14271-5_1

tongue was not English; Gandhi was from Gujarat (Gujarati language) and Mandela from Transkai (Xhosa language), but they were both able to master other languages.[1] This demonstrates the power of language in terms of the spread and diffusion of concepts and ideas related to liberty and civil rights issues.

In this respect Gandhi was very clearly seeing the law and language issue in terms of power when, in 1908, he rejected English on ideological grounds. At the turn of the century, English was not the language of international law, and the upturn in the role and status of English as the global language of law and international rights was yet to come. At the time he found it painful to use before courts of law because, as long as India was still subject to the British crown, it was the language of the colonizer.

> To give millions a knowledge of English is to enslave them… Is it not painful thing that, if I want to go to a court of justice, I must employ the English language as a medium: that, when I became a barrister, I may not speak my mother-tongue, and that someone else should have to translate to me from my own language? Is this not absolutely absurd? Is it not a sign of slavery? (Gandhi 1958, p. 5; in Crystal 2012, p. 124)

The question of language and liberty is vital in the many fields of legal study and practice: for the legislator, magistrate, and for the victim and the accused. This importance is widely recognized, as it appears on the Internet and in comments on the importance of language and freedom in a judiciary trial:

> Mandela's ability to speak English may well have saved his life. He defended himself in court during the Rivonia Trial in 1963 where many expected the outcome to be the death sentence, yet he received a sentence of imprisonment for life. During the speech, he also comments on his respect for British political institutions and the 'independence and impartiality' of the British Judiciary. Whilst he accepted that English and Afrikaans – both official languages of South Africa were the languages of the oppressors, it is clear that he revered English for its association with education and liberty.[2]

The initial part of his speech is now history:

> "I am the First Accused. I hold a Bachelor's Degree in Arts and practiced as an attorney in Johannesburg for a number of years in partnership with Oliver Tambo. I am a convicted prisoner serving 5 years for leaving the country without a permit and for inciting people to go on strike at the end of May 1961."

It was delivered as a statement from the dock at the opening of the defense case in the infamous Rivonia Trial, Pretoria Supreme Court, 20 April 1964.

---

[1] Ismail Ayob is another Indian man of law in South Africa who had an active role in human rights cases during the anti-apartheid regime, defending and representing South African political prisoners. On account of his Indian heritage, he could not attend university and had to move to London (London School of Economics). He returned to South Africa to practice as an attorney. He was also connected to Nelson Mandela.

[2] Xhosa was Mandela's mother tongue. He learnt English while attending a religious Methodist school. Afrikaans came at a later stage, during his 20 years imprisonment. The first Bible translation into Xhosa was in 1859. Today Xhosa is used with English to teach in primary schools (https://lingos.co/blog/nelson-mandela-the-importance-of-language-and-freedom/. Access July 23, 2014).

Mandela was found guilty on four charges of sabotage and was sentenced to life imprisonment. Material now available online, and the widespread use of international legal English mean that there is now a level of comprehension and communication that at the time was impossible.[3]

From a linguistic point of view, the use of the term 'dock' may be ambiguous to non-native speakers of English. In a non-specialized context, 'dock' is an international term meaning waterfront or wharf. However, in this context, it is the place where the accused stands. In Italian it corresponds to 'banco degli imputati,' as opposed to 'witness box,' 'banco dei testimony.' Not all legal dictionaries consulted recorded these terms (BLD,[4] FDG, PEG et al.). Maybe they were deemed too obvious. The term 'docket' or 'judicial record,' an informal record in which a judge or court clerk briefly notes all the proceedings and filings in a court case, is, however, entered in some dictionaries: for example in is entered in the 'old', but not the 'modern,' American *Black's Law Dictionary* (BLD) and it is not entered in the British Oxford Dictionary of Law (OXDL).

To conclude this introduction and link the framework of research to a cross-thematic approach, recent events offer examples of the use of English as a legal weapon and as a tool in terrorism. The posting of a video of American freelance photographer, James Foley's assassination is an example of the use of English in the context of mock justice. From a linguistic perspective, the appalling sequence emphasizes the use of English for legal or criminal purposes to instantly communicate the message to a global audience on the Internet. English forensic linguistics is used to determine the identity of the speaker, and the use of multicultural London English tends to produce ambiguity, as can be seen in this excerpt from the online news:

> Language experts say the masked killer sounds like a man in his 20s who was raised or educated in Britain. John O'Regan, a linguist at the University of London's Institute of Education, said the militant spoke with a 'multicultural London English' accent but with more formal standard English pronunciation, suggesting that his words denouncing American actions in the Middle East had been carefully scripted.[5]

---

[3] See also African National Congress (http://www.anc.org.za/show/. (Access 8 August 2014).

[4] See abbreviations for dictionaries used. BLD refers to *Black's Law Dictionary*. Henry Campbell Black (1860–1927) first published his magnum opus in 1891. The dictionary has evolved over its six unabridged editions and was compiled using modern lexicographic principles, based on previous dictionaries. Ours is the 1998 edition. It contains the Constitution of the United States. The Editor-in-Chief of the new edition is Bryan A. Garner, author of *A Dictionary of Modern Legal Usage* (2d ed. 1995), *The Elements of Legal Style* (1991), *Guidelines for Drafting and Editing Court Rules* (1996), all areas which indicate an increasing concern with the legal writing and usage. West's Law Dictionary (WLCD) is based on BLD.

[5] http://news.nationalpost.com/2014/08/21/ Access August 23, 2014.

References

Azar M (2007) Transforming ambiguity into vagueness in legal interpretation. In: Wagner E, Wouter W, Cao D (eds) Interpretation law and the construction of meaning. Springer, Berlin, pp 121–137

Beke T (2014) Litigation communication. Springer, Berlin

Cao D (2007) Translating law. Multilingual Matters, Clevedon

Crystal D (2012) English as a global language, 2nd edn. Cambridge University Press, Cambridge

Jakobson R (1966) Saggi di Linguistica Generale. Feltrinelli, Milan

Joseph J (1995) Indeterminacy, translation and the law. In: Morris M (ed) Translation and the law, American Translators Association, scholarly monographs series, vol 8. John Benjamins Amsterdam, pp 13–36

Katan D (1999) Translating cultures. An introduction for translators, interpreters and mediators. St. Jerome, Manchester

Morris M (ed) (1995) Translation and the law. American Translators Association. John Benjamins, Amsterdam and Philadelphia

Nelken D (1996) Comparing legal cultures. Hanover. Dartmouth College Library, New Hampshire

Taylor C (1998) Language to language. A practical and theoretical guide for Italian/English translators. Cambridge University Press, Cambridge

Tiersma PM (2012) A history of the languages of law. In: Tiersma PM, Solan LM (eds) The Oxford handbook of language and law. Oxford University Press, Oxford, pp 13–26

Van Hoecke M (2002) Law as communication, EALT series 4. Hart Publishing, Oxford

Chapter 2
Theoretical Concepts

The first thing we do, let's kill all the lawyers
William Shakespeare, *Henry IV*

2.1 Preliminary Observations

Translation efforts are constantly thwarted by lack of equivalents, missing slots (Joint Stock Company), shifts in meaning, diverging systems, desemantization (the generalization of meaning of a sign) and symmetrical void. This may affect some of the most common words such as the Italian *cambiale,* which has government stamp duty, whereas an IOU 'I owe you' has no equivalent, or the Joint Stock Company, which does not correspond to the Italian Società per Azioni, SpA. In English 'spa' (/Spa/) has a different meaning, although in is also used in Italian in the sense of 'stazione termale.' Mistakes featured in international headlines are no excuse for mistakes courtroom interpreting.[1] As noted, the first letters and words in legal dictionaries have triggered endless discussions with experts and colleagues: for example, letter-A terms entered in legal dictionaries such as *abigeato* (cattle stealing) and *abduzione* are asymmetrical to their English equivalents in denotative and connotative features. 'Abduction,' extends to other conceptual domains of application, as in C.S. Peirce's science of signs. There are also questions concerning the indeterminacy of law and language, and the relationship between different legal systems. The challenge increasingly facing legal communication is the usage and spread of varieties of English around the world and the idea that international legal English is not strictly 'international law.' The two different areas of study and

[1] Italian headlines featured the interpreter's failure to simultaneously translate former British Minister Geoff Hoons at court hearings on Finmeccanica and bribery (http://www.dagospia.com/rubrica-4/business/du-iu-spic-inglisc-figura-merda-italia-processo-77727.htm), when the interpreter publicly stated that: Il perito chiamato, dopo aver tentato di arrampicarsi sugli specchi, ha confessato: «Traduco a senso». E alla fine, tra l'imbarazzo generale, la testimonianza è stata rinviata di una settimana. Con il testimone che con grande humor british [sic] ha commentato: «Mi scuso di non essere io in grado di parlare italiano» (M.T. Conti, May 23, 2014 in http://www.ilgiornale.it/news/interni/linterprete-non-capisce-e-ministro-blair-non-pu-testimoniare. Access 24 May, 2014).

R. Masiola and R. Tomei, *Law, Language and Translation*,
SpringerBriefs in Law, DOI 10.1007/978-3-319-14271-5_2

action do, however, overlap and are mutually reinforcing factors in language globalization. Moreover, this implies that any legal lexicography cannot be severed from conceptual meaning, interpretative practice and the hermeneutic motion, or shun legal reasoning and legal theory (Atria 2002, 2012).

In its first section, the study starts with such postulates on theories of meaning and interpretation. In the second section it moves from concepts to specific lexicon and semantics. In Chap. 4, it progresses to a comparative case study of a specific theme. Subsequently, the historical roots of 'tribal crimes' such as horse stealing from Apaches, and consequent Indian wars are briefly outlined in order to identify language issues and compare variations in cross-cultural legal issues.

The aim isn't to provide solutions, but to raise issues, problematize and to be a caveat against oversimplified approaches to the interpretation and translation of legal systems and jurisprudential doctrine. The comparative cross-cultural thematic and linguistic approach has been useful as it can highlight variations in place and time with regard to the perception and evaluation of crimes, ranging from myth to brigands and cowboys and Indians. What do the Wild West outlaws, Apaches and Comanches, Billy the Kid in Lincoln County (New Mexico), Australian duffers, and African rustlers have in common? This brief surveys aims at stimulating reflection and investing more in the socio-cultural and linguistic implications when crimes become 'trendy' again and the death penalty is enforced as has recently been the case of South Sudan where 'blood compensation' has been called for. In Jamaica in June 2013, a 'higgler' was 'chopped to death.'

The question of international law and civil rights issues is examined in the final section. Legal instruments, international negotiations, treaties and memoranda are all subject to translation and interpretative issues. There is no declaration of war, no subsequent treaty of peace and cooperation that is drafted in one language. English is used for international bilateral treaties and constitutionally in most post-colonial states. It is used as an international language in bilateral treaties or multilateral treaties. A simple premodifier or the concept of 'possession' and its interpretation can change the course of world history, as it did in the case of the 'conquest of America.' The history of colonialism, Western expansion and territorial acquisitions developed on the basis of linguistic mediation, translation and interpretation of such treaties, right or wrong. What is interesting in terms of understanding the dynamics is not so much the 'whys,' but the 'hows' and detecting the language mechanisms that caused things to go wrong.

2.2 Introductory Topics: From Theory to Theme

In its introductory second chapter, this survey highlights aspects of language and law as a realm that is integral to every culture, such as language interpretation and translation of the language of the law and theoretical concepts. The study moves on to an applicative third chapter, where it focuses on the problems of definition and multilingual lexicography. This section addresses the dynamics of communication and translation as a cross-cultural phenomenon. A conclusive fourth chapter features comparative thematic analysis of a criminal offense as reported in the media and as perceived and constructed in terms of cultural and legal discourse. The common topic is that of 'cattle stealing' in different languages, cultural traditions and legal systems, and its synchronic and diatopic variation. The issue is not without relevance: in Italy it is no longer an individual crime, only an aggravating circumstance of theft, and the dramatic global increase in violence and bloodshed as a result of this crime is hardly reported in the European media. Little information is given about a crime caused by hunger and depression. Criminals are sentenced to death (Texas and Arizona); 'blood compensation' has been made legal (regions of South Sudan), and digital media promotes the use of emotional language. In Jamaica, as already noted, a 'higgler' was 'chopped' to death, and New Zealand's, South Africa's and Australia's innocent farmers are 'down on their knees.' When borders are crossed, when the crime is subject to international law or in the case of extradition, the question of language and interpretation is determinant in all phases of the law, in defining jurisdiction and subsequently the applicable norms. The notorious case of the two Italian marine officers detained in India has been presented by the media as highly intricate and impenetrable legal proceedings (national, federal, state, international, etc.).

The final chapter is based on the problem of international treaties in translation. It is aimed at stimulating a debate and raising awareness of the dangers and perils in international relations and conflicts. It examines several case studies where, in the course of history as well as in more recent times, negotiations and conflict resolutions were put at stake by erroneous interpretation and translation. Language, law and cultural systems are three factors that have a global impact—especially in light of tragic events and videos posted by Isis terrorists.

2.3 Concepts and Definitions

The European advocacy of 'harmonization of the law' within the multilingual jurisprudence of the ECJ (Lòpez-Rodrìguez 2004; Falkner et al. 2005; McAuliffe 2012, pp. 200–216) is one of the great challenges of the global millennium, and is based on a new 'world order' (Wagner et al. 2007). In a perfect world, the role of 'the law,' shunning any theoretical limitations, is to serve the community, the people and individuals alike, communicating across cultures, nations and linguistic barriers (Gibbons 1994). It may seem, however, that the 'world order' is constantly challenged by 'word disorder' and constantly thwarted by linguistic barriers. Legal communication is at risk when semantic polysemy, indeterminacy and ambiguity fail to provide clear-cut definitions and equivalents in bilingual or multilingual lexicography or in translation or multilingual statutory interpretation (Bennion 2002).

As further observed, the question of ambiguity and indeterminacy, which call for a good deal of intentional flexibility in terms of application in legal contexts (Bix 1993), may also be a stumbling block in linguistic translation (Joseph 1995;

Azar 2007; Poscher 2012). Accordingly, the present study refers to the major Western systems and some specific 'words' in legal language and their conceptual and implied meanings (Benjamin 1989; Harris 1980). This highly specific domain covers the well-founded discipline of legal philosophy (Rottleuthner et al. 2007), theories of meaning and translation (Guethner and Guethner-Reuter 1978), the 'effability hypothesis of translation,' the 'exact translation hypothesis' or ETH (Katz 1978)[2] and accommodation. Conceptual dictionaries for translation in the field of law (Šarčević 1989) would, however, be useful if also extended to legal philosophy and linguistics.

The Latin and Roman juridical traditions of civil law have played a primary role in promoting the dissemination of its statutory principles and corpus, combining the law of the Republic and the Roman Empire in those countries where this system is implemented. The other major system and tradition is that of English common law. Today, the two systems co-exist within the mosaic of the world scenario on a globalized scale, where the Latin words also pertaining to common law and used as such in English acquire supranational currency. The use of Latin words extended to the linguistic area of Eastern Europe epitomizes this trend and presupposes common European and Latin roots.

Some key terms have been selected on the basis of semantic dissymmetry ranging from taxonomic concepts and hyperonyms or superordinates, e.g. 'rule' (Nida 1964, 1975) as observed in this chapter. In the following sections, the focus is on a comparative theme (cattle stealing) and its variations in register (interlingual) in European languages and legal systems, and range of synonyms within English (varieties of English). On the basis of the definition of the crime, there are social and cultural dynamics, which impact equally on the law, language and media resonance. The question is not 'beyond conjecture' for although Europe considers cattle stealing a crime belonging to a legendary past featured in western movies, it is subject to the death penalty (Texas, Arizona) and 'blood compensation' is called for (South Sudan) against a background of tribal warfare and famine in contemporary Africa.

2.4 Materials and Methods

Partly inspired by George Steiner's 'hermeneutics' and translation, and Pietro Perlingieri's concept of 'subsumption,' this second chapter highlights issues related to conceptual juridical lexicon. Cultural filters and linguistic constraints due to different traditions (Ehrmann 1976), the main trends from the earliest surveys on law and linguistics (Mellinkoff 1963) and the recent updates (Tiersma 2012) have

[2] See Jerrold Katz's reference to 'effability hypothesis' and the 'principle of expressibility' versus Willard Quine's celebrated thesis of 'indeterminacy' of translation, as an example of skepticism (1964, pp. 61–81). The latter, in his 'theory of perspectives or theory of belief' relies upon the axiomatic point that meanings are not merely relative, but that they are absolutely *indeterminate* with respect to our system of rational knowledge (Rosini 1992: 169). See further sections.

been taken into account.[3] The field of legal translation (Morris 1995; Cao 2007) is now an accredited academic discipline together with forensic linguistics (Coulthard and Johnson 2007, 2010). At the same time, there are also countless contributions to comparative law (De Cruz 1999). In view of the existing approaches, the current aim is to provide further insights into the discipline of comparative legal linguistics (Mattila 2006) from a cross-cultural and multilingual perspective (Bahtia et al. 2003). The methods rely on comparative thematics and translation studies and theories. Materials are authentic and based on a study of cattle stealing.

Examples focus on instances of polysemy, asymmetry, register in usage, significance and definition when diachronic and diatopic variation is consistent, even within the same legal system, let alone between the major legal systems used around the world today (Ehrmann 1976; David and Brierly 1985). The adopted approach examines the lexicon and conceptual meaning in literary citations and legal discourse. The examples range from inquiries into the conceptual and epistemological lexicon to more recent colloquialisms or newly coined 'trendy' words, and the degree to which translating them produces shifts in meaning and stylistic register. Dictionaries, whether specialized or multilingual, have their limitations.

There are theoretical key concepts (*sussunzione*) in Western juridical traditions, not even recorded in bilingual law dictionaries.[4] The increasing trend in acronyms (DASPO in Italian), means that semantic shifts and variation in language usage often occur. These terms coexist in legal templates in the stylized and frozen legal language. There are numerous examples of terms with many meanings and of several terms with one meaning. An interesting case is the term 'posse.' In legal English, 'posse' deriving from *posse comitatus* comes from medieval Latin, meaning 'to have power, signifying':

> An assemblage of the able-bodied male inhabitants of a county, except peers and clergyman. The sheriff of the county could summon it either to defend the county against the King's enemies or to enforce the King's writ. (WLCD 1988)

The Italian equivalent entered in West's multilingual dictionary (WLCD) has no institutional equivalent of a 'county.' The item that is entered is *potere di una contea* (power of a county). The German definition is far more helpful 'Hilfspolizei.'

What is more interesting for the mediator, however, is the fact that the term is frequently used in connection with Jamaican culture and music (e.g. yards,

---

[3] Items featured are 'intentionalism, interpretation versus construction, judicial discretion, legislative intent, linguistics, literary theory, methods, multilingual texts, purpose, teleological, translation errors, uniform interpretation and application of EU law' (Tiersma 2012: 634). There is hardly any reference to current Italian legal culture and no index reference for 'private law.' The work offers a massive tome and a globally comprehensive guide to systems. See also the pioneering work *Lexicography and Conceptual Analysis* (Wierzbicka 1985).

[4] The question of translatability of the term was raised by Italian researchers and scholars (*LawLab: Communicating Legal English,* University of Foreigners, Perugia, October 2013) and the ensuing debate focused on the fact that it was not entered in dictionaries. The real challenge for us was calling to account an interdisciplinary approach, as the term is recorded in other domains of science.

dancehalls) and as a loan word in European youth jargon. It is not recorded in Jamaican (JED) or Caribbean dictionaries of English (DEC), but it is recorded in the British Collins Dictionary (CED), where it has the same historical meaning as above, but also refers to the US legal meaning of 'possibility' (*in posse*); slang: a Jamaican street gang in the U.S.; 'informal': 'a group of friends or associates.'

Legal English features a vast array of animal-based metaphors, in most cases linked to the market and stock-exchange, e.g. porcupine provision, pork-barrel legislation, shark repellent, leonine contract, blind tiger, cats and dogs, and many others.

Localization and semantic asymmetry in Western languages constitute filters in understanding and communicating legal lexicon. The concluding remarks highlight the complex quagmire of legal translation (i.e., Italian and English), essentially because of the different types of English and the use of English as the international legal language of private law and criminal offense (British, American, Australian, New Zealand, Jamaican, South African). Moreover, despite the fact that English lexicon and, in particular Western legal lexicon, derives from Latin and Roman law, there are still variations. Specifically, variations refer to usage and perception of meaning, as well as the main difference in the taxonomy in the diverse legal systems. In addition, Latin-based lexicon is beguiling to speakers of Romance languages and civil law experts (Mattei 1997; Merryman et al. 1994).

2.5 A Comparative Thematic Approach

The question of Latin, Italian and legal English is based on cultural, linguistic and semantic relationships related to the problem of meaning, significance and translatability within the United Kingdom, as in the case of Scotland (see also Dossena 2005). Therefore, examples are based on diachronic, diatopic variation of civil law and common law lexicon. The way in which such lexical items are institutionally used, contextualized and defined in literature constitutes an initial corpus. The data and items analyzed include legal repertoires, mono-bilingual and multilingual dictionaries, online glossaries; news and media reporting has provided material for investigation and a possible database. Method used was a comparative approach of one specific theme, as perceived and narrated in the media mainly across anglophone areas.

In a globalized world that speaks English as the lingua franca and where international legal English is a vehicle for international communications and 'world order,' the present contribution aims to underscore the problem of 'word disorder.' There can be cases where professionals, stakeholders and the lay audience will not understand that a one-to-one translation is a mere utopia, and total interlingual symmetry is hardly possible and is subject to cultural filters and linguistic constraints. Moreover, there are adjustment techniques, adaptation, modulation, borrowing and explanatory glosses to enhance comprehensibility.

On a more practical basis and in money matters, 'business is business,' and in conflict of law, e.g. in Italian 'diritto internazionale privato,' contracts are often drafted in templates. Contracts are subsequently translated into two or more different languages (e.g. Italian, English, plus other Western or Eastern languages). Low legal linguistic profiling, erroneous interpretations and misconceptions, and linguistic manipulation seriously jeopardize the whole judicial hearing and international credibility, thus causing international friction or worse. Flukes, flounders and lame ducks are the body of evidence here, such as recent cases that have caused embarrassing interruptions during courtroom hearings, thus impairing and distorting courtroom debate.

As noted, one of the red alerts and *caveats* when faced with Latin-derived legal English lexicon is that of ambiguity and 'false friends' based on 'acoustic agreement' or homonyms, homography, and allonyms. As opposed to polysemy and multiple meanings for one term, in this case there are several terms for the same 'meaning,' but with different provenances and different contextual denotations and connotations. The impasse caused by extended polysemy, satellite meanings and clusters of meaning (Nida 1964, 1975) in the field of multilingual legal lexicon is another area of possible confusion in translation and communication. Moreover, there are diachronic shifts in meaning and significance through borrowing and adaptation in the receiving systems as featured in further sections. The cross-cultural variation and perceptions of *abigeato* and 'cattle rustling' are then analyzed (Italy, the Americas, Australia, New Zealand, Africa, India).

Factors and concepts like 'indeterminacy' and hermeneutic interpretation are highlighted in the following sections, in order to illustrate the comparative-thematic approach to international crime.

2.6 Conceptual Meaning: Indeterminacy and 'Subsumption'

To introduce this section and link with development of subsequent topics, we consider the concept of indeterminacy, its significance in legal and language theory and its impact on legal communication:

> The translation of legal texts of any sort, from statute laws to contracts and courtroom testimony, is a practice that is at the crossroads of the three areas of theoretical inquiry: legal theory, language theory (broadly defined to include the interests not only of linguistics but of rhetorical and textual theory as well), and translation theory. [...] In a sense, these theoretical enterprises have been catching up with what working translators, lawyers, and field linguists have known for centuries: that all three of these enterprises founded in language are fundamentally indeterminate (Joseph 1995, p. 13).

The author concludes his introductory remarks on the topic by observing that 'translation always falls short of its goal' in terms of conveying meaning and style (this is questionable). It emphasizes the fact that the meaning of words is 'never fixed,' and what is more interesting for the present investigation is that the 'law is subject to interpretation; the idea that it is carved in stone is only an illusion'

(Joseph 1995, p. 14). Again, what may arise here is another reflection: that of 'flexibility' and interpretation and its correlation with the dynamics of diachronic interpretation and variation in language usage. This brings us to a related theoretical and applicative issue: the principle of *subsumption*.

One of the epistemological issues the Western scholar of law systems and lawmakers is likely to face in drafting, understanding and implementing normative principles bridging the super-ordinate domain of constitutional law and civil law is the principle of /subsumption/. In the hierarchy of legal epistemology, /subsumption/ is a conceptual sign with a precise definition and based on the hermeneutics of interpretative practice. Bilingual or multilingual legal lexicography does not seem to document it. Let's look at some authoritative examples:

The pioneering *Piccola Enciclopedia Giuridica* (Parisi 1959) omits it in both the English and the Italian entries. The seminal reference book for American and British law, *Black's Law Dictionary* in its updated edition of 7,500 terms, follows suit. There is no mention of the concept in the American Translators Association monograph *Translation and the Law* (Morris 1995), not even in the subject index. Furthermore, it is not dealt with in the *Oxford Handbook of Language and Law*, (Tiersma 2012), which does however contain exhaustive classification for the lexeme 'interpretation.'

'Subsumption' is one conceptual and epistemological term the Italian legal researcher may want to examine in the different legal languages of the European Union in order to see how it correlates with Roman law and common law and check possible institutionalized equivalents.

The present investigation aimed to localize items in Roman law concepts, using evidence based on definitions and multilingual or bilingual lexicography. One legal dictionary available to Italian practitioners is, however, structured on an English-only base with lexemes and concepts defined in Italian (De Franchis 1984). It lists obsolete Latin terminology, but again there is no trace of 'subsumption.' Nor is the term recorded in the British *Osborn's Concise Law Dictionary* (OCLD 2013) or the American *Black's Law Dictionary* (BLD 1996), reflecting the divergence of the common law systems and constitutional-based systems, and corresponding conceptual lexical omission in recording.

In the extensive introduction (265 pp) to the Italian-English dictionary, de Franchis laments the lost cause of finding matching equivalents, as indicated by his repeated use of linguistic *prétérition*. He observes that the task is impossible: 'La mancanza di un sistema di equivalenza concettuali tra l'ordinamento italiano e quello inglese e nordamericano.' The two juridical cultures diverge:

> Il termine *civil law* impiegato in questa ricerca non indica il *diritto civile*, ma corrisponde al significato e all'uso fattone attualmente nelle opere di diritto comparato italiane e straniere e nella prassi internazionale. Con esso si intende la tradizione giuridica del continente europeo di derivazione romanistica... (Franchis 1984, p. 23).

/Subsumption/ is also not recorded in the recent *Oxford Dictionary of Law* (Law and Martin 2013), an updated source of terminology for systems based on English law. The widely consulted multilingual Italian edition of *West's Law Dictionary*

(WLCD) is based on the cited unabridged *Black's American Dictionary*, and likewise omits the term. As the concept is based on Roman law and constitutional legal systems, the juridical systems featured therein may have required the entry, i.e. Italian, French, Spanish, German should have required it.

A quick online search, however, shows the term contextualized in legal principles, and a non-specialized dictionary has the definition for the verb /subsume/: 'to consider an instance of something as part of a general rule or principle (C 16 from New Latin */subsumere/* from Latin sub + sumere = to take).' The noun has no reference to constitutional norms.

Giovanni Perlingieri featured the term in a pioneering essay on interpretation and the hermeneutic motion in the seventies, and it has been reflected on in more recent essays on the principles of constitutional norms and doctrine, mainly by German contributors.

Another perplexing and problematic issue for readers and translators of either common or private law is the confounding nature of English grammar, and the fact that a term which may appear ordinary can conceal a very specialized technicality of legal decisions. One example of this is the noun 'set-aside' and the verb 'to set aside.' This is recorded in some in legal dictionaries (BLD, OLD), and omitted others (OCD). While it may be obvious for the native speaker, it is trickier for a non-native dictionary user:

> **Set-aside**, noun. "something (such as a percentage of funds that is reserved or put aside for a specific purpose" (BLD).

Things may have a more defined application in a specific context, such as the European Union. So when the item is entered in a non-specialized British dictionary (CED), its connotations expand beyond the purely legal doctrine. The verb 'to set aside' however, even if related to procedural law, is also not always entered in monolingual legal dictionaries. The term is highly technical:

> **set aside** (Of a court) to annul or vacate (a judgment, order, etc.) <the judge refused to set aside the default judgment> (BLD)[5]

2.7 Validity in Interpretation and Hermeneutics

As noted elsewhere (Rosini 1992, p. 169), there are philosophical 'schools' that take different approaches. As summed up in E.D. Hirsch's work *Validity in Interpretation* (1962), focusing on the Hegelian influence on the German philosophical tradition has challenged the debate and stressed the author's intentionality, as opposed to deconstructive criticism and the Barthian 'death of the author' trends in literary interpretation. Basically Hirsch distinguishes between:

---

[5] This note is indebted to observations on translation made by Dr Angela Taticchi and my colleague Francesco Duranti while we were discussing comparative systems and linguistic issues.

1. intentionality, as in Edmund Husserl (phenomenological approach)
2. the possibility of sharing linguistic signs and meanings
3. the hermeneutic tradition from Friedrich Schleiermacher to Hans-Georg Gadamer.

When his work came out in America in the sixties, the debate on the question of interpretation divided 'schools of thought.' Some 50 years later, the challenge in terms of constitutional interpretation and the authoritative stance lies in relying on the author's intentions. As recognized, in terms of positive criticism this may apply to the framers of the constitution or authors of legislation.

This approach would also be valuable in the area of legal interpretation, yet this analysis of the constitution would actually 'set aside the idea of a dynamic and 'living' constitution' (Van Meter 2001). The following notes illustrate the opposing dynamics if authoritative meaning is juxtaposed to social and community significance:

> He makes a vital distinction between 'meaning' and 'significance.' Meaning ultimately is dependent on authorial intent. A written document can only MEAN what the author intended it to mean. The author may have been unskilled or even incompetent in presenting his/her ideas, but the meaning forever remains what it meant at creation. Significance, however, is the personal, social and cultural context in which any reader's reaction to the written text takes place. A given written text may have significance for an individual or community that goes beyond the original author's intent. This significance may, in some sense, have no direct connection to original intent. It remains valid as 'significance' but not as 'meaning.'[6]

The enactment of meaning and belief consequently correlates here to the principle of cooperation, which aims to preserve the authorial spirit, or 'imprint.' In the case of the law, reference is akin to the authoritative spirit of the law, corpus or codex and applicative aspects of 'effability' and adaptation of the spirit of 'translation of the law,' as a legal procedural practice, and to 'real' authors on the topic and intertextual references. Intertextuality may extend to the law in translation (Orr 2003) and is used as a genre itself (Gotti 2012, p. 66).

At this point reference should be made to George Steiner's hermeneutics as emphasized in his seminal *After Babel: Aspects of Language and Translation* (1975). In relation to the 'hermeneutic motion,' Steiner postulates a fourfold transfer of meaning and translation (trust, aggression, incorporation, restitution). An act of 'trust' is an act that binds the interpreter of the law to the preceding compiler. If correlated to bilingual legislation and the infiltration of Roman law written in legal Latin into other cultures and languages, the following quote on 'trust' is particularly relevant for both the legislator and translator. They both have to interpret. So this approach combines the two roles of the man of the law and the interpreter:

> The hermeneutic motion, the act of elicitation and appropriative transfer of meaning, is fourfold. There is initiative trust, an investment of belief, underwritten by previous experience but epistemologically exposed and psychologically hazardous, in the meaningfulness, in the 'seriousness' of the facing or, strictly speaking, adverse text. [...] All

[6] Randall K. Van Meter. 'Difficult but groundbreaking' (8 July 2001). Paperback review. Online. (amazon.com. Access: 11 September 2014).

> understanding and the demonstrative statement of understanding which is translation starts with an act of trust. This confiding will, ordinarily, be instantaneous and unexamined, but it has a complex base. It is an operative convention which derives from a sequence of phenomenological assumptions about the coherence of the world, about the presence of meaning in very different, perhaps formally antithetical semantic systems, about the validity of analogy and parallel (Steiner 1975, p. 297).

There are impacting factors and cultural dynamics that are mandatory when faced with the meaning of juridical lexicon and its 'translatability' and 'quality in translation.' It may be useful at this point to refer to a list of categories of meaning derived and adapted from Leech (1974, p. 91):

1. Conceptual meaning, related to logic, cognitive and denotative content. It is also called essential, and all six other meanings are peripheral.
2. Connotative meaning, based on communication in relation to what language refers to. It is the communicative value of an expression beyond the purely conceptual.
3. Stylistic meaning, based on what is communicated from the social circumstances of language.
4. Affective meaning, which refers to the emotive associations evoked in the listener, reader, speaker, etc.
5. Reflected meaning arises when a word has more than one conceptual meaning, and relates to what is communicated through association with words occurring in context with another word. Reflected meaning and collocative meaning involve interconnection.
6. Collocative meaning, the communicative value that an expression has by virtue of what it refers to, over and above its purely conceptual content.
7. Thematic meaning refers to the structure and organization of a message in terms of marked order and emphasis.

In legal discourse and judicial hearings and translational semantics, all these may occur equally. The question of conceptual interpretation of meaning is the core meaning, and the others are constellations or satellites. Such is the case of constitutional norms and how they relate to the enactment of civil law (Perlingieri 2013). 'Subsumption' may be theoretically defined as a concept, and then enacted on a performative level. The term has currency in logic and Charles Sanders Peirce's representational logic and extends to algebraic computation, deriving from terminological representation languages for knowledge representation systems.

At the lexical level of language, reflected meaning arises when a word has more than one conceptual meaning or multiple conceptual meanings. In such cases, while responding to one sense of the word we partly respond to another sense of the word too. The following sections focus on aspects of meaning and applications.

References

Atria F (2002) On legal reasoning. EALT Series 3. Hart, Oxford
Atria F (2012) Legal reasoning and legal theory revisited. Int J Semiot Law 25:537–577
Azar M (2007) Transforming ambiguity into vagueness in legal interpretation. In: Wagner E, Wouter W, Cao D (eds) Interpretation law and the construction of meaning. Springer, Berlin, pp 121–137
Bahtia V, Candlin C, Gotti M (eds) (2003) Legal discourse in multilingual and multicultural contexts: arbitration texts in Europe. Peter Lang, Bern
Benjamin A (1989) Translation and the nature of philosophy. A new theory of words. Routledge, London
Bennion F (2002) Statutory interpretation: a code. Butterworths, London
Bix B (1993) Law, language and legal determinacy. Clarendon Press, Oxford
Black's Law Dictionary (1996) West Group USA, New York
Cao D (2007) Law in Translation, Multilingual Matters, Clevedon
Coulthard M, Johnson A (eds) (2007) An introduction to forensic linguistics: language in evidence. Routledge, London
Coulthard M, Johnson A (eds) (2010) Routledge handbook of forensic linguistics. Routledge, London
De Cruz P (1999) Comparative law in a changing world. Cavendish Publishing, London
David R, Brierley J (1985) Major legal systems in the world today. Stevens, London
Dossena M (2005) Apud acta: the contribution of Latin to scots legal vocabulary. ESP Across Cultures 2:47–57
Ehrmann W (1976) Comparative legal cultures. Prentice Hall, Eglewood Cliffs
Falkner G, Treib O, Hartlapp M, Leiber S (eds) (2005) Complying with Europe: eu harmonisation and soft law in the member states. Cambridge University Press, Cambridge
De Franchis F (ed) (1984) Dizionario Giuridico Inglese-Italiano. Law Dictionary English-Italian, Giuffré
Gibbons JB (ed) (1994) Language and the law. Longman, New York
Gotti M (2012) Text and Genre. In: Tiersma P, Solan L (eds) The Oxford handbook of language and law. Oxford University Press, Oxford, pp 52–66
Guethner F, Guethner-Reuter M (eds) (1978) Meaning and translation philosophical and linguistic approaches. Gerald Duckworth, London
Harris JW (1980) Legal philosophies. Butterworth, London
Joseph J (1995) Indeterminacy, translation and the law. In: Morris M (ed) Translation and the law, American translators association, scholarly monographs series, vol 8. John Benjamins, Amsterdam, pp 13–36
Katz JJ (1978) 'Effability and translation'. In: Guethner R, Guethner-Reuter M (eds) pp 191–234
Law J, Martin EA (eds) (2013) Oxford dictionary of law. Oxford University Press, Oxford
Lòpez-Rodrìguez AM (2004) Towards a european civil code without a common european legal culture: the link between law, language and culture. Brooklyn J Int Law 29(3):1195–1220
Leech G (1974) Semantics. Penguin, Harmondsworth
Mattei U (1997) Three patterns of law: taxonomy and change in the world's legal systems. Am J Compar Law 45:5–44
McAuliffe K (2012) Language and law in the EU: the multilingual jurisprudence of ECJ
Mellinkoff D (1963) The language and the law. Little, Brown and Company, Boston
Merryman JH, Clark Avid S, Haley JO (1994) Civil law tradition: Europe, Latin America and East Asia. The Mitchie Company, Charlottesville
Van Meter R (2001) Difficult but groundbreaking (8 July 2001). Paperback review. http://www.amazon.com/review/
Morris M (ed) (1995) Translation and the law. American translators association. John Benjamins, Amsterdam
Mattila H (2006) Comparative legal linguistics. Ashgate Publishing Company, Aldershot

Nida E (1964) Toward a science of translating. Brill, Amsterdam
Nida E (1975) Language structure and translation. Stanford University Press, Stanford
Orr M (2003) Intertextuality. Polity Press, Cambridge
Osborn's Concise Law Dictionary (2013) Sweet and Maxwell, London
Parisi GA (1959) Piccola enciclopedia giuridica italiano-inglese-italiano. Giuffrè, Milano
Perlingieri P (2013) Constitutional norms and relations to civil law. The Italian Law Journal, ESI, Napoli
Poscher R (2012) Ambiguity and vagueness in legal interpretation. In Peter MT, Lawrence MS (eds) The oxford handbook of language and law. Oxford University Press, Oxford. p 128–144
Rosini RM (1992) The transmigration of myth meaning and translation'. In: Lewandowska-Tomaszczyk B, Thelen M (eds) Translation and meaning, vol 2. Faculty of translation and interpreting RHM, Maastricht, pp 169–178
Rottleuthner H et al (eds) (2007) A treatise of legal philosophy and general jurisprudence (V vols.) Springer, Dordrecht
Šarčević S (1989) Conceptual dictionaries for translation in the field of law. Int J Lexicogr 2–4 (277):293
Steiner G (1975) After babel. Aspects of language and translation. Oxford University Press, Oxford
Tiersma PM (2012) A history of the languages of law. In: Tiersma PM, Solan LM (eds) The Oxford handbook of language and law. Oxford University Press, Oxford, pp 13–26
Wagner A, Wouter W, Cao D (eds) (2007) Interpretation, law and the construction of meaning, collected papers on legal interpretation in theory, adjudication and political practice. Springer, Berlin
West's Law and Commercial Dictionary (1988) Zanichelli, Bologna
Wierzbicka A (1985) Lexicography and conceptual analysis. Karoma Publishers, Ann Arbor

Chapter 3
Definitions and Applications

'Why may not that be the skull of a lawyer?
Where be his quiddities now, his quillities, his cases, his tenures, and his tricks?'

(William Shakespeare, *Hamlet*, V, I, 99)

'When I use a word,' Humpty Dumpty said, in a rather scornful tone, 'it means just what I choose it to mean—neither more nor less.'
'The question is,' said Alice, 'whether you can make words mean so many different things.'
'The question is,' said Humpty Dumpty, 'which is to be master—that's all.'

Lewis Carrol, *Through the Looking Glass*

3.1 Functions and Contexts

In terms of language functions and textual typology, there are more clear-cut categories, where, for example, a legal text or law correlates to the 'vocative function' or the German-derived 'appellative' function, in the sense that it targets an 'adressee,' and it is aimed at inducing a certain behavior (to do or not do something). The author-centered approach is seen as an 'expressive' function, and the informative function relies on what the text actually says and the information it provides. These categories have been expounded in the field of translation studies, notably by Reiss (1971) and Newmark (1982). The interaction between textual typologies and multimedia is one important framework of analysis in legal communication and translation.

In introducing this theoretical section, it is worthwhile considering how assumed virtual severance between meaning and significance is counteracted by interaction with three basic functions of language (Rosini 1988, pp. 298–302). These may coexist and simultaneously interact, although in varying degrees. A more recent approach, using the triadic 'author-text-message' model, is offered by the concept

R. Masiola and R. Tomei, *Law, Language and Translation*,
SpringerBriefs in Law, DOI 10.1007/978-3-319-14271-5_3

of legal discourse and discursive practices in the courtroom. This is yet another sector of legal practice. It entails legal interpretation on the one hand and legal interpreting on the other. Modern legal interpreting considered in terms of its international impact and cross-cultural dynamics was epitomized by the Nurnberg trial and other Nazi criminal trials. This situation posited crucial questions not only to the translators and interpreters, but also to the jury.

As with the notorious Nixon Watergate case, they all relied on certain concepts, their values and beliefs, and their translation. Dissociation through itemization, the adding of further technical details and figures (i.e. precization), are key elements in defining concepts as argued with the opponent in a trial or interview as in the following section. Intertextuality and citation are used between the two opponents as defense and attack moves.

3.2 Legal Discourse: 'Obstruction of Justice'

Dissociation as an argumentative technique is a relevant part of legal discourse. As noted in one particular study:

> Only in dissociation a more or less profound change is brought about in the conceptual basis of an argument: one single unitary concept is separated into two new concepts. An example is the separation of the concept of 'law' into new concepts: 'the letter of the law' and 'the spirit of the law' (Van Rees 2005, p. 53).

Obstruction and 'obstructing justice' may thus be split, where concept is severed from the evil act.

Nixon used the technical term 'obstruction of the course of justice' as a counter-argument in the televised Watergate interview with David Frost (May 4, 1977); as a lawyer he couldn't resist explaining the meaning of the term to his interviewer, who was not a lawyer.

The terms used in this interview highlight code and register variations in American and British English usage. The non-Anglophone political commentator may be baffled by some terms, as such items may vary along the continuum of legal lexicon and common speech: liable, wrongdoing, hush money. The term 'political containment,' used by Richard Nixon as an understatement for political effect, is a new coinage that defined 'obstruction of justice' as being a criminal offense. Nixon loads his defense with pseudo-technicalities and legal small talk with the intention of masking his wrongdoing and abuse of presidential power. He is rebutted and contradicted by David Frost, and then Nixon refers to 'quibbles.' Nixon tries to grapple his way through the divide between the concept of 'legality' and its correlation to the American constitution and presidential powers. This also entails 'obstruction of justice.' The interviews, along with numerous comments, are available online with video transcripts. What follows is a brief excerpt of online commentary on this specific definition from the May 4, 1977 interview:

> Frost also *probed* Nixon about directing his aides to have the CIA ask the FBI to stop following certain leads in its investigation of Watergate. [...] Nixon later tells Frost in the interview, 'It was a grievous mistake to have gotten the CIA involved in this thing.' Still, in this exchange, Nixon insists this was not a *criminal act*. But Frost replies that Nixon knew that criminals would be protected. Nixon objects and tries to qualify, but Frost persists: '*An obstruction of justice is an obstruction of justice if it's for a minute or five minutes...*'
>
> In the televised portion of the interview, at this point, Nixon appears shaken.
> He then says his '*absence of motive*' precludes any criminal intent.
> But Frost jumps on that and surprises Nixon, suggesting the ex-president's knowledge of the law is incomplete. '*The law states,' says Frost, 'that when intent and foreseeable consequences are sufficient, motive is completely irrelevant.*' (emphasis added)[1]
> Nixon says nothing and appears uncomfortable.

Nixon was put on the defensive and made a clumsy 'repair' move, observing that Frost did not have the legal expertise for definitions. It is based on semantics and contexts:

> Nixon is almost immediately on the defensive, explaining the difference between a 'good' cover-up and a 'bad' cover-up—you see, *it's only a cover-up if it's covering up something illegal*, and *it's only obstruction of justice if justice is successfully obstructed.* Frost is at his absolute best in this segment, skillfully negotiating the spin of his formidable opponent, who refers to him, without sarcasm, as 'the attorney for the prosecution.' For his part, Nixon certainly plays the part of the defense attorney, frequently adding in extra language and saying things like 'I would argue that I meant...' as opposed to just saying 'I meant.' Frost asks tough questions ('Why didn't you stop it?').[2]

The whole discourse and defense is based on rhetorical skills such as the use of linguistic 'hedging' as in the above examples, distancing from the core matter with technical details and definitions. The result is a meaning of 'obstruction of justice' that connotes power and presidential office.

3.3 Lexicography and Translation

In terms of dictionary definition, the entry 'obstruction of justice' is omitted from the British OLD (2013), and in the British OXLD it refers to 'obstructing a police officer' (2009). In the Italian English FLD (1984), it is recorded with misleading denotation referring to '*resistenza a un ordine dell'autorità giudiziaria*,' the latter defining 'obstructing process.' The same is given for parliamentary strategies of *obstructionism*: 'obstructing justice' → with vague Italian equivalents. To be more exact, *ostruzione, ostruzionismo* refers to 'obstructive conduct' in parliamentary debates. A more adequate term would be 'intralcio al corso della giustizia,' as contextualized in the Watergate scandal and subsequent impeachment.

---

1 http://www.pophistorydig.com/topics/tag/nixon-obstruction-of-justice/ (Access 11 September 2014).

2 http://www.pophistorydig.com/topics/tag/nixon-obstruction-of-justice/ (Access 11 September 2014).

The three main distinctions: to obstruct justice, obstruct proceedings of legislature, and to obstruct process, pertain to different legal contexts and actions. In the first instance it is exemplified by the constitutional context of Watergate and possible impeachment; the second case refers to parliamentary practice to counteract opponents, and the case of 'to obstruct process' may not be easy for the non-native expert to distinguish, as it refers to 'serve process' as legal duty or court order (warrant). They are entered in a multilingual dictionary (WLDC) respectively as:

German: *Behinderung der Rechtspflege*
Spanish: *Obstrucciòn de la acciòn judicial*
French: *Entraver le cours de la justice*
Italian: *Ostacolare il corso della giustizia*

Regarding semantics of meaning, the interpretation of conceptual legal lexicon is thus performed along a continuum model ranging from legal theory to interlinguistic translation. While 'intra-system' attitudes advocate 'binding authorities' to support legal writing (Strong 2010), in the case of 'interlinguistic or 'intersemiotic' mediation, any kind of matching between systems can only be approximate if the 'binding authorities' for a translator/mediator are simply lexicography. In his *Language to Language*, Chris Taylor argues that:

> The overriding consideration in the legal language of any idiom is that it be flawless and therefore not betray the fundamental rights of any person or group. The consequent scrupulous attention paid to making sure that legal text is hermetic and unambiguous is one of the main reasons for its, at times, seemingly impenetrable, syntactic complex nature, full of apparent redundancy. For translators this is both a blessing and a curse in that they cannot make mistakes, but the guidelines are rigid; there is little or no room for creative interpretation (Taylor 1998, p. 126).

Again, this brings up the underlying antinomy of a theoretical 'absolute' correspondence of words and law, and the impossible symmetry, convergence and 'sameness' as derived from clusters and constellations of meanings. On the other hand, the language of the law is 'the correct language.'[3]

With reference to bilingual or multilingual entries, 'obstruction of justice' is a case in point. Consequently, the question of 'validity in interpretation' impacts also on translatability and multilingual lexicography. There are points of confusion between similar terms in English and Italian because of the intricacies of English and changes in institutionalized meaning from Latin and Anglo-Norman derivations. The term *statement of defense* has no relation to a possible equivalent syntagm in Italian, *dichiarazione della difesa.* In legal Italian it corresponds to *replica del convenuto* (not a 'convener').

The approximation of diverse procedural systems and the cautious nature of legal decision making is thus constantly questioned by the challenge of identifying legal authorities and harmonizing conflicting definitions for the interpreter and

[3] The language in which the law is written and structured is considered the prescriptive model into which national languages is cast, as in the case of King James Bible (see further).

mediator, who are expected to evaluate applicability and equivalence in the constant interaction between language, law and system, as well as the resultant translational issues in practical application (see also Olsen et al. 2009).

This survey advocates an international and multidisciplinary approach, whether the 'implied reader' is a linguistic mediator or a non-Anglophone legal expert. Once the equivalent is found, consistency is paramount.

3.4 Conceptual Lexicon: Liberty, Crime and Felony

There is an interpretative 'choice' and there is also a 'choice' of words (Gibbons 1994). In international contracts, the choice of legal system and language is a crucial issue as a contract can be drafted in two or three languages, and this was the case even before globalization (Reese 1962). Juridical culture and the Italian hermeneutical tradition must inevitably come to terms with issues of linguistic translation, adaptation, commentary and definition. In particular, the question of interpretation correlates with statutory texts and commentaries on norms, when the role of written sources and authoritative citation is mandatory.

Conversely, on a lexico-semantic level, there is a 'core meaning' with possible constellations of meaning rotating round that core meaning. Interpretation and performative action of the lawyer and interpreter may be subject to shifts. Although 'natural' and constitutional law should ideally correspond one-to-one in meaning and word, there may be different hierarchies in perceived meanings and lexicalized concepts.

There are paradigmatic variations in cognitive and conceptual domains in English, for example, for the words 'liberty' and 'freedom,' or stemmed diversification along the axis of politics, policies, policy and polity. There are several surveys based on 'distributional techniques' and componential analysis (Nida 1964, pp. 96–118). In terms of translatability and concept, the two different items coexisting in English as 'liberty' and 'freedom' inevitably poses pragmatic and stylistic issues for translators. Understanding cultures through their keywords is an important issue alongside the diachronic variation of meaning as outlined by Wierzbicka (1997, pp.129–136) in her cross-cultural and comparative study on 'freedom' as a culture-specific concept in Latin, English, Russian and Polish. Wierzbicka recognizes the lack of serious cross-linguistic analysis. The passage is cited here as it underscores the untranslatability of legal terminology. Some items are dealt with in later sections of this study (bail, democracy):

> In particular, what is lacking in the philosophical literature is an analysis of 'freedom' and related concepts undertaken from a cross-linguistic perspective – an analysis which would be able to reveal, in a rigorous and methodological way, the similarities and the differences between concepts related to 'freedom' which have been lexically encoded in different languages, and which are often assumed to be simply identical.
>
> Philosophers, political scientists and students of law are usually aware of the untranslatability of relatively technical concepts such as 'bail,' 'warrant,' 'custody,' 'solipsism,'

> 'determinism,' 'parliament,' 'oath' and 'democracy.' There is, however, much less awareness that non-technical concepts, such as those encapsulated in the English words freedom, justice and truth, are also language-specific. An awareness is also lacking of the fact that words encode certain conceptualizations rather than any objective 'pictures' of reality, or that the same situation or state of affairs can be differently construed for their purpose of linguistic encoding (Wierzbicka 1997, pp. 125–126).

In a recent analysis defining the question of freedom and liberty, Cardinal Eugenio Ravasi featured the question of 'liberty' (in the sense of freedom) juxtaposed to 'evil.' Ravasi noted the Indo-European roots of the term are *peh* present in its apophonic variants in *feh, be, fi,* which have extended into different languages. It is present in the Greek term *Eleutheria*, and in the Latin *Libertas*. Ravasi's argumentation was to contextualize the theme of freedom against that of evil, as present in the Lord's Prayer in Latin *libera nos a malo*, this being an invocation to deliverance (deliver → liberate) from evil and all forms of evil (war, injustice, famine and plague)[4].

Once the concept of liberty within intellectual lexicon of European languages is defined, it is important to technically define evil actions, felony, crimes, wrongdoing, illicit behaviors, misdemeanors and larceny. The Frost-Nixon interview examined in the previous section is emblematic of the power of lexicon in relation to criminal law in context. As noted, the more common charges against blacks (*felons*) were *felony* charges: arson, murder, rape and burglary, in some cases punishable by death. The question is not merely a technical quibble, but may be an intended distortion and manipulation, as with the terms 'felon' and 'felony' that were adopted to refer to a law dating back to the time of immediate abolition of slavery in the USA, in order to bar the black vote. The crime was revamped and tweaked for the notorious electoral purge in Florida in 1997 by a resurrected 1868 law that prevented felons from voting.[5] It was difficult for international analysts to translate the term, as being rather obsolete, it is not recorded in bilingual dictionaries. A 'felon' was somebody who was condemned for 'felony,' and this implied crimes such as treason and murder. Capital punishment and forfeiture of assets were the consequences.

As in other instances, e.g., 'larceny,' when there is no symmetrical and direct lexeme, the entry is omitted in most bilingual Italian dictionaries. The terms are, however, entered in dictionaries that are based on American dictionaries (WLCD) with generic equivalents such as 'thief.' As a serious crime may be punished with a death sentence, it is logical to have the full entry in the U.S., whereas in the UK the term is obsolete. For 'larceny,' an Italian dictionary records this is common-law definition: 'E' con questo termine che si definisce il furto nella common law' (FDG). The same dictionary defines 'felony' using other English terms: "Era detto così in passato un delitto capitale come quelli di *treason* e *murder* (FDG). A British dictionary (OXDL) remarks on the obsolescence of the term once punishable by the death sentence, and the obsolescence of the term *larceny*. Current American

[4] '*Libera nos a malo–La libertà*' conference held at the International University 'Stranieri', Perugia, September 13, 2014.

[5] See documentary *Unprecedented. The 2000 Presidential Election*, directors Richard Pérez and Robert Greenwald (2004).

legislative lexicography recording the death penalty (BLD) negatively impacts on European scholars and students[6]

> *Felony*: Formerly, an offense more serious than a *misdemeanour*. *Since 1967 the term has been abandoned* (although it is retained in pre-1967 statutes that are still in force) and the law formerly relating to misdemeanors now applies to felonies.
> *Felony*: A serious crime usually punishable by imprisonment for more than one year *or by death*:
> *Larceny*: Formerly (before 1969), theft. Larceny was more limited than theft and required an asportation (carrying away of property).
> *Misdemeanor*: Formerly (i.e. before 1967), any of the less serious offences as opposed to felony (emphasis added).

The term larceny (Larceny Act 1916) is substituted by 'theft' (Theft Act 1968). It is, however, currently used in Australian legislation, especially referring to cattle stealing (see below, Sects. 4.3 and 4.4) and in American dictionaries (BLD), with its derivatives (larcenist, larcenable, larceny by bailee, grand larceny, petty larceny, etc.).

The term 'misdemeanor' also reveals omissions in bilingual dictionaries. There is a Woody Allen film *Crimes and Misdemeanors* translated into Italian as *Crimini e Misfatti,* the latter term emphasizing criminal action in the lay perception, outside the technical area. It is recorded in bilingual dictionaries as 'reato minore,' a minor offence (DEL).

An important legislative reform came in 2005 with the Constitutional Reform Act, providing for a Supreme Court to take over the functions of the House of Lords, in the UK. Several domains and juridical disciplines have been subject to changes including new rules and amendments in national, European, and international legislation based on treaties and conventions. The legislative reforms in public acts and in private laws of 1969 have a bearing on terminology and English language referencing in the UK in terms of communication and subsequently of translation. This may not apply to all former Commonwealth countries, where obsolete terms coexist with national expressions (e.g. Australian 'larceny and duffing,' American 'felony,' etc.), or where informal expressions are widely used ('mugging' for larceny) with a marked socio-linguistic denotation. The old words are retained on the basis of the frequency of the crime of 'asportation,' for example, of large quantities of animals, e.g. cattle, where grazing space is vast. This further exacerbates translation difficulties. However, in terms of reforms the seventies coincided with the rising momentum of the 'plain language movement' (see below).

If instances of legal taxonomy are examined, it can be seen that superordinates and their symmetrical relations between languages are difficult to map (Cruse 1997). One 'classic' example is the contextualization of the word 'code,' which in Italian and English, as well as in other Western languages covers some fourteen

6 Negative reaction (dismay and frustration) has been experienced at all time by the authors when teaching postgraduate courses (2008–2014; University for Foreigners, Perugia, Italy).

meanings, from 'formalism' to 'lexicon' as in the 'taxonomic code of botany.' The word 'rule' is another term that has both technical and common meanings and applications.

3.5 Hierarchy in Meaning: 'Rule'

The concept and componential hierarchy of the English word 'rule,' when applied to translation equivalents is, however, more problematic. In fact, a notorious 'false friend' is the term 'rule' and 'rulings,' from English to Italian, as in 'parliamentary rulings' pertaining to decrees, decisions and not to 'norms,' which is often misunderstood as 'regolamenti parlamentari, regole del parlamento.'

The illustration in Fig. 3.1 (Nida 1964, p. 110), refers to/rule/and features semantic contrasts in the English language based on 'patterns of ambiguity' and 'points of resolution' between such ambiguities, as Eugene Nida noted in his epoch-marking work on Biblical translation, *Toward a Science of Translating* (1964, pp. 110–111).

This is not the only domain in which the law and media feedback 'make things happen': the prominence of legal cases recently highlighted in the media and press releases thrives on a combined typology of legal communication, and calls for more adequate tools for analysis and interpretation. In contrast to the word 'spirit' (limited to the spirit of the law), the word 'rule' is noted by Nida (1964), p. 109 for its semantic diagram of structural contrasts. The word 'rule' includes several features and is better understood when legal concepts and lexicon are introduced. There are different correlations between noun (N) and verb (V), as illustrated by T.

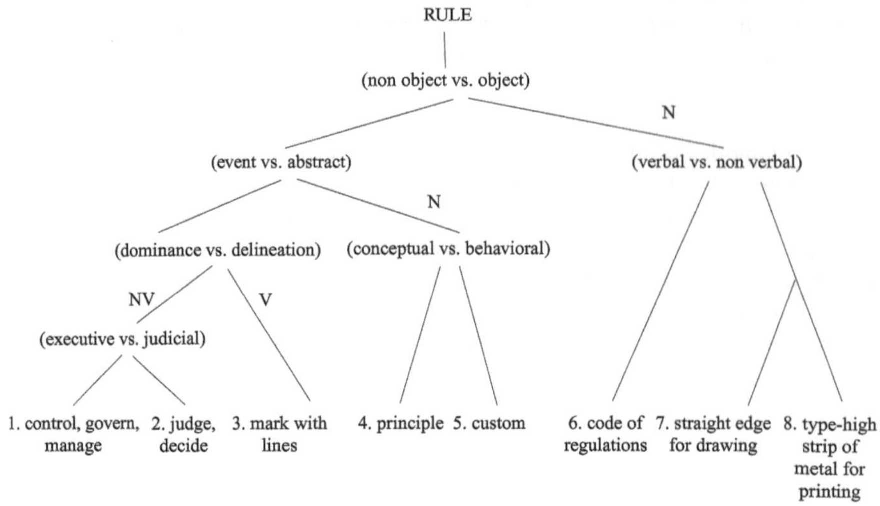

Fig. 3.1 Nida 1964, p. 110 (Reference is main text p. 40, 2.5, in part two)

The semantic 'markers,' which are salient for legal lexicon, feature the following binary items, but do not always overlap with Italian or other Western legal lexis:

'conceptual' vs. 'behavioral' → nouns principle vs. custom
'executive' vs. 'judicial,' → verbs 'to control, to govern, to manage, to judge, to decide.

3.6 International Legal English

As noted, one feature of law and language that equally hampers English and Italian juridical language is the die-hard presence of archaisms and obsolete lexicon. These are matched by the flurry of neologisms and an influx of modern crimes for which the media invents acronyms, compounds and mafia-style jargon, sometimes with foreign words. The phenomenon can be seen at different levels—national and global, European, American, Chinese, Indian and African. Crime knows no frontiers, and is a dynamic factor within society and its expressive modality and literature on the problem of the growing world food crisis. International legal English and the globalization of law via conventions and international principles of law fit punishments to the crimes. The language of law and the administration of justice are reported on by the media, combining technical terms with jargon and slang expressions related to delinquency, especially in the case of direct quotations or interviews derived from forensic discourse and courtroom interactions.

The many specific domains wherein legal English is used vary not only in terms of juridical culture and systems, but also in terms of language and translation. There is legal English as used in the European Community and constitution, which is subject to multilingual legislation. There is English in its major international varieties (Canadian, Australian, U.S., New Zealand, etc.) and there is English as used in Scotland and the relevant juridical system (Dossena 2005; Bugaj 2006).

Global and local media report news related to international crimes and court proceedings. Debate at an institutional level overlaps with citations and interviews on the topic and quite often there translation acts as a bridge to international communication. Reporting and news translation may occur simultaneously, when the press and social forums engage in dialogue and institutional debate when a bill is passed. The law defines the crime and labels it. One example is the case of femicide, a term for gendered murder. Obviously enough, English is the language of international communication and criminal justice and laws are reported in English. English as a legal language has its peculiarities, which make it difficult to understand and translate in both directions. The paradox being that it was precisely the language of the law that gave structure to formal written English, and that this occurred via translation. Such is the case of the King James Bible or *Authorized Version* (1611–1636), as it was translated from Hebrew into English. Another paradox is the fact that under the assumption of 'modernity' this ancient and ossified style has been maintained in its clichés and cryptic formulae, thus rendering legal English a matter of mystery for the layperson and non-native speaker alike.

Considering the current migratory trend of the global population and the need for an international language in international law, this works to the detriment of communication and accounts for loss in meaning and translation at all levels in judiciary proceedings, constitutional laws, civil rights and asylum laws. The next sections briefly outline some salient features, where the 'plain language movement' in many Western countries is calling for a reform and simplification of legal language. This meets the needs of public institutional dialogue with local and national communities. Communities have been steadily becoming more multilingual, hosting unprecedented linguistic varieties and minority groups within Europe and around the globe.

3.7 Plain English, Law and Literature

It was not until the seventies that concerted efforts were made to counteract cryptic legal language. The abstruseness of legal language and the power that resides within the administration of justice in a language precluded to outsiders has been the subject of countless literary parodies in the history of Western literature, from François de Rabelais to Jonathan Swift, from Charles Dickens to Jeremy Bentham. Plain language or the 'plain language movement' has spread to non-Anglopone countries, like Italy and Spain. One milestone was the widespread reaction to David (Captain) Mellinkoff's *The Language and the Law* in 1963, a damning critique of the age-worn defense of legal technicalities used by lawyers and scholars. More recently members of the European Union's translation service launched the *Fight the Fog* campaign.

The language of law, often referred to as 'legalese,' represents a specialized language or register. It is actually a language within a language with an obsolete system of phrasing and ritualized formulae pertaining to the many fields and subfields of law and jurisprudence. The special language of scientific disciplines (i.e., medicine, engineering, chemistry) features a constant influx of new words—a trend that indicates the linguistic permeability of the global scientific community. The ever-increasing number of technological innovations and patents have meant that scientific language is unquestionably English-derived and anglicized in form (Rossini 1998). The same dynamics do not apply to the law and language, where national and international communities need to understand the language in order to abide by the laws. The plain language movement (Adler 2012, pp. 1967–1973) acts for the community as the recipient of the laws resulting from the globalization of legal discourse (Gotti 2009). It is intended to have considerable positive effects on communication at home and abroad. Mark Adler in his lifetime crusade is adamant: the problems of legalese can be cured without significant change in language; almost none of the impenetrable language adopted by traditionalists is required by the law. Adler uses the lethal weapon of common sense and plain reasoning:

> The ideas expressed in legal documents (in contrast to those of theoretical science) will rarely, if ever, be so counter-intuitive as to be beyond the reach of clear explanation. And it is undesirable that they should be, as such complexity would make the obligations difficult to comply with and so defeat the purpose of the documents (Adler 2012, p. 83).

We live in a diasporic world where English is used in Europe and throughout the world, beyond former Commonwealth countries and British dominions, and where multilingualism includes English, as in India and on the African continent. Translation may be affected in many areas, such as legal terminology, multilingual judiciary systems and courtroom interactions. The plain language movement is yet another important factor relevant to communication and institutional accessibility (Asprey 2010). English is not the only language that uses legalese; the language of the law may be equally cryptic in other European languages, as what is discussed in the native tongue may be incomprehensible to a general audience. There is a social need to reduce and minimize the ambiguity of the legal jargon. Plain language is aimed at ensuring correct communication that would enhance translatability, reduce risk of loss in meaning and maximize clear comprehension of the law in a multi-cultural and multilingual context.

In particular, due to the high level of specificity, the translation of legal texts and their specialized terminology pose several problems not present in other subjects, such as when a person does not understand what crime he/she may have committed, or why he/she signed a contract that cannot be honored, or what bail means (see Australian Aborigines, Sect. 5.4). Back in the seventies, linguists like Crystal and Davy stigmatized it as 'one of the least communicative of all uses of language, but also as far removed as possible from informal spontaneous conversation.' (1969, pp. 193–194). Crystal further criticized how 'legal language is always being pulled in different directions' (Crystal 2003, p. 374).

Clearly, the use of the language and its specific characteristics can vary in different domains and contexts, some of which are more formal than others, with a selective usage of prescriptive deontics and epistemic modality (Garzone 1999, 2007).[7] The range of legal communication and discourse, independent of nation and language, may vary from technical subject-centered definitions and debates, spoken exchanges in court instructions to jury members, interpersonal communication (members of the legal profession), the press and institutional media, diplomacy and international bodies. It may also require the use of mediators such as interpreters and translators, court transcribers and readers of transcripts. In this case activity is both oral and written. In this regard, Crystal examined a sensitive case of linguistic analysis and transcription involving an Internet pedophile and the victim. This situation is constantly faced by forensic linguistics and the focus has to be on analysis of conversations and recordings of a specific ritual code of questionings; applied linguistics is of no help here (Crystal 2011, pp. 122–123).

[7] The author adopts a functional approach in a pragmatic perspective (1999, pp. 391–408). Other authors focus on techniques of 'legal transposition' or in French 'transposition juridique' (Didier 1990, p. 9; Crépeau 1995, pp. 51–61; Šarčević 1997, pp. 12–13).

Written legal texts may include case law, law reports or prescriptive legal texts. In most European languages (Italian, English, French, etc.) they feature long and complex sentences with unclear patterns of subordination and coordination. International institutions follow suit here with breathtakingly long sentences. United Nations resolutions are made up of a single sentence, but often stretching to hundreds or thousands of words. This is because they follow well-established drafting rules and templates: starting with the name of the authorizing body, followed by a preamble with unfinished clauses ending with a comma ('reaffirming that,' 'deeply concerned about'...). The style is protocol-like, with formulaic archaism used as causal, restrictive and temporal connectives, such as *hereinafter, henceforth, whence, heretofore, aforethought*, etc. typical of legal English. As for technical verbs in judiciary procedure, a descriptive periphrasis would be more user-friendly: verb, *to darraign*: to settle a controversy; to clear a legal account; noun, *surrejoinder*: the answer by the claimant to the rejoinder by the defendant, made by the claimant, in answer to the defendant (Williams 2004, p. 112).[8] These terms are not always recorded in bilingual dictionaries and are recorded in English legal dictionaries as being obsolete in legal practice. The widely used term 'plaintiff' with its cognate 'pleading' have been substituted by 'claimant' (Italian *querelante*; defendant: *convenuto in giudizio, imputato, querelato*) and 'claim form' after the introduction of the Civil Procedure Rules in 1999.[9] There are also instances of the opposite being true, such as the case of common-usage phrasal verbs that are used in legal terminology, and imply an institutionalized praxis. Constant updating of the definition and lexicon is *conditio sine qua non*. Examples here are from the British law dictionary (OXDL). The first lexeme is quite frequent in common language with many meanings. Here it is relevant in commercial contracts:

> 'to set-off': *n*. 1. a monetary cross-claim that is also a defense to the claim made in the action by the claimant. 2. The deduction of monies owed against sums due to be paid. Many commercial contracts *contain express terms prohibiting set-offs*.
> 'to set aside' or setting aside: An order of the court canceling or making void some other order or judgment or some step taken by a party in action. In certain circumstances judgment in default may be set aside or varied under Part 13 of the Civil Procedure Rules (OXDL)

On the other hand there is an imbalance and dissymmetry in style and register with Latin-derived terms. Latinate terms are quite familiar to speakers of neo-Romance languages such as Italian, Spanish and French, and at the same time they are abstruse to lay Anglophones. There is a massive presence of foreign words, especially from French and Latin, due to centuries of Norman domination of England in the sphere of

---

[8] Surrejoinder Italian: "*replica dell'attore alla duplica del convenuto*". (WLCD) *Duplica* is Italian legalese for the common word *replica*. Omitted in other dictionaries.

[9] Most Italian-English dictionaries consulted do not record the difference, which is partly given in WDCL. The difference in terminology and obsolescence of terminology due to reforms is duly recorded in the Oxford Law Dictionary, and, even if less precisely, in American West's. Italian equivalent claimant/plaintiff is *querelante* with no difference; and for defendant: 'imputato, convenuto, citato in giudizio,' depending on physical presence in court.

law and government. This is also common in many fields of science (botany), applied arts and crafts as noted nearly a century ago by Albert Baugh in his seminal *History of the English Language*. In legal English there is an abundance of lexical loans and adaptations from Latin, Anglo-Norman and French, and these have been preserved in the formation of binomials. These binomials may even appear as formulaic lists representing reduplication, and have no counterpart in translation into other languages. Translators are aware of this, especially those working with remote cultural legal systems. For example 'null and void' is translated in Chinese as 'to no effect' → *wuxiao* (Cao 2007, p. 90). However, there is a rationale behind this reduplication and doublets and triplets in English; they convey all-inclusiveness and normally have one meaning, as in these three examples: cease, desist and be at end; obey, observe and comply with; bear, sustain and suffer.[10]

In English, the spread of Roman law and diffusion of Latin adapted to English law developed into law Latin. Conversely, there is a tendency to revive Latin terms in the new body of laws and constitutional body of countries of the post-Soviet area (Tiersma 2012; Mattila 2012). Moreover, the judicial system has codified the use of Latin expressions no longer in use in Italian or French. Semantic shifts occur in terms such as: *habeas corpus* which is actually a 'writ' used to challenge the detention of a person; or the French term *Guillotine,* which is a 'procedure' to speed up legislation. The quest for clarity is comparable to the campaign for 'plain legal English' (Wagner and Cacciaguidi-Fahy 2006).

On the whole, legal texts suffer from excessive wordiness, largely as a result of the ancient custom of paying clerks by the page, which meant that they deliberately made legal documents as long as possible. There is also a lexical redundancy and syntactic expansion to avoid possible ambiguity, and although the effect may be disorienting it may also have a prescriptive function and deter breach of contract, as in this typical English contract form, where alliterations abound:

> ...it is their intention to hereby *fully, finally, absolutely and forever settle* according to the provisions of this Agreement any and all *liabilities, claims, disputes and differences* which may exist or may have ever existed between them...(Cao 2007, p. 88).

These constructions are not only used in legal texts but also in other written registers, such as scientific discourse or journalism, and once again we have to consider the specific contexts in which legal texts are drafted. The use of the passive form can be useful e.g. to avoid specifying the actors involved. Another trend is converting action verbs into nouns, and this actually occurs in institutional legal communication across the media of all Europe to the point of ludicrous constraints on parliamentary lexicon into implausible '-azation.'

On April 26, 1998 the legal language used in the British courts and decades of traditions were swept away by a new set of rules published in a document by the Lord Chancellor's Department. As we can see, in this document, old Latin and French law terms were replaced by 'plain legal English' terms. Despite of all the

---

[10] Robert Dick gives a full list of two-word and three-words strings (1985, pp. 126–127). Cited in Cao (2007), pp. 89–90.

efforts to make legal language easier to understand, present-day legal English continues to be highly specialized and distinctive, stimulating debate and research. On the other hand there is a question of style and literary tradition of textual genre. There are alliterations and assonances, which are part of an oral tradition of poetry and drama. In addition, there are instances where the colloquial and the legal style may coexist, as in the case of legal transcriptions.[11] Some of the major trends and themes in the history of Western literature and cinematography evolve around the staging of a trial. European literature and translation theory and practice have developed alongside plots constructed around a law theme, from the Bible and the Gospels to the *Law and Order* TV series. The legal cases cover the question of law and justice, freedom and emancipation, and crime and punishment. *The Merchant of Venice*, *Mutiny on the Bounty*, *The God Father*, *The Crucible*, *The Scarlet Letter*, *The Caine Mutiny*, *In the Name of the Father*, *The Quiz Show*, *To Kill A Mocking Bird*, *Les Misérables*, *A Tale of Two Cities* and *Amistad* are just a few of the British and American works adapted into films. Mainstream legal thrillers and mafia books are a resource for translators. Forensic rhetoric is yet another powerful Western tradition with all its oratorially coded strategies. Ampflication, in the art of forensic rhetoric for instance, includes *commoratio* (a finishing touch), *hypotyposis* (descriptive sketching), *enthymeme* (accumulation of details and superlative itemization) and *epiphrasis* (accessory repetition), all aimed at emotional effects and maximizing interest and suspense.[12] One can avoid supercilious Latin- or Greek-derived terms and use ‘plain language’: the spoken word, idiomatic connotations and a captivating voice will do more to rivet the audience and the jury. Variations of English and Anglophone-based pidgins and creoles are fathomless verbal resources (Crystal 2012). Presumably there is a readership more interested in the law of God than in ‘plain language,’ and alongside the ‘plain language’ movement, implementation of multilingual drafting and translation into minority languages will be useful to the ‘plain citizen.’ The question of ‘plain English,’ lingua franca English and international legal English needs further in-depth survey and its global spread needs monitoring, given the fact that forensic mediators currently have only inadequate resources at their disposal.

Moreover, there is the question of the language of the law as a literary heritage. The King James Bible can be seen as a molder of modern written English, even if the English used overlaps with that of other Bibles, such as Tyndale and Wycliffe in 1388.

---

[11] David Crystal’s comments on a courtroom clerk’s record (1615) on a case of alleged defamation. The language is a fascinating mix of legal and colloquial styles, at one extreme using such formal and formulaic locutions *as the said deponent* (i.e., the person making the deposition) and at the other reporting everyday vocabulary (*to doe with, whore*) and syntax (*hast minde, wentes to leache, thancke mee for it*). The two styles meld in such phrases as *as farre as this* deponent ever heard, which presumably is a transcription of ‘as far as I ever heard’ (2004), p. 336.

[12] See Garavelli (1997), pp. 234–237. English explanation in brackets is the author’s (Masiola).

Doing away with it would be just as unthinkable as doing away with Shakespeare's use of law language. David Crystal in his remarkable book *Begat*, on the influence of the King James' Bible and legal authorization, observes that:

> ...when people talk about the King James Bible introducing various expressions into English, it doesn't mean that they always originated there. Rather, it gave them a widespread public presence through the work being 'appointed to be read in Churches.' Despite its popular name being the 'authorized version,' the work was never authorized in any legal sense. But no other translation reached so many people over so long a period as King James. And this probably explains why so many of its usages entered public consciousness (Crystal 2010, p.9).

The recitation of law rituals and formulae, and the reading of passages from the Bible was an oral practice, relying on prosodic device. The patterns of imitation and resonance are testified by song lyrics, and not only hymns (*Fame and Fortune*): 'aid and abet'; 'devise and bequeath'; 'goods and chattels.'

This knowledge and information is preposterous when an Aborigine, a Maori, or an American Indian is expected to understand the foreign language (English) being spoken to him or her when sentenced to death or life-imprisonment. In the U.S. there are some brilliant lawyers and civil rights activists who are Indian Americans (Pawnee Kevin Gower). This topic will be examined in Chap.5. There may eventually be cases where legal English *tout court* is not a pandemic curse and 'plain language' the panacea. Plain language is certainly desirable and mandatory in individual transactions, and in dialogue-driven change in the public sphere (Masiola and Tomei 2013). The globalized world is also a diasporic world of displaced communities and migrants. Multilingual and multi-ethnic communities or minority groups living within the legal system of the 'ruling class' must be enabled to abide by its laws.

There are, however, cultural and historical situations accounting for the maintenance of legal instruments in style and format, such as supranational legislation, international treaties and national constitutions. In international law contracts language choice is determinant (De Vries 1962). Simplified drafting is intended to counteract the frenzied jargon of bureaucracy in the various norms each citizen comes across in daily life. More than making things clear, adequate communication of the law should entail translatability and cross-cultural mediation.

References

Adler M (2012) The plain language movement. In: Tiersma PM, Solan LM (eds) The oxford handbook of language and law. Oxford University Press, Oxford, pp 67–86

Asprey M (2010) Plain language for lawyers, 4th edn. Federation Press, Sydney

Bugaj J (2006) The language of legal writings in 16th century Scots and English: an etymological study of binomials. ESP Across Cultures. 3:7–22

Cao D (2007) Translating law. Multilingual Matters, Clevedon

Crépeau P A (1995) La Transposition juridique. In: Snow G and J Vanderlinden dir. Français juridique et science du droit. Bruylant, Bruxelles

Cruse D A (1997) Lexical semantics, 2nd edn. Cambridge University Press, Cambridge
Crystal D (2003) The cambridge encyclopedia of the english language, 2nd edn. Cambridge University Press, Cambridge
Crystal D (2010) Begat: The King James Bible and the English Language. Oxford University Press, Oxford
Crystal D (2011) Internet linguistics. Routledge, New York
Crystal D (2012) English as a global language, 2nd edn. Cambridge University Press, Cambridge
De Vries H (1962) Choice of language in International Law Contracts. In: Reese WLM (ed) International contracts: choice of law and language. Oceana Publications, New York pp 14–22
Didier E (1990) Langue set langages du droit: étude comparative des modes d'expression de la common law et du droit civil, en français et en anglais. Wilson and Lafleur, Monreal
Dossena M (2005) Apud acta: The Contribution of Latin to Scots Legal vocabulary. ESP Across Cultures 2:47–57
Garavelli BM (1997) Manuale di Retorica. Bompiani, Milan
Garzone G (1999) The translation of legal texts. A functional approach in a pragmatic perspective. Textus. English Studies in Italy. 12. Tilgher, Genoa. 391–408
Gibbons JB (ed) (1994) Language and the law. Longman, New York
Gotti M (2009) 'Globalising Trends in Legal Discourse. In: Bartol D, Duszak A, Izdebski H, Pierrel JM (eds) Langue Droit Société Language Law Society. Special Issue of Cahiers DNPS (Dictionnaire des notions politiques et sociales des pays d'Europe centrale et orientale), 5:351–365
Masiola Rosini R (1988) Questioni Traduttive. Campanotto, Udine
Masiola R and R Tomei (2013) Gender in Blackness. Stereotyping in Children's Literature, Media and Political Discourse. International Journal of Cross-Cultural Studies and Environmental Communication, 147–164
Mattila H (2012) Legal vocabulary. In: Tiersma P, Solan L (eds) The oxford handbook of language and law. Oxford University Press, Oxford, pp 27–38
Newmark P (1982) Approaches to translatioon. Pergamon, Oxford
Nida E (1964) Toward a Science of Translating. Brill, Amsterdam
Olsen F, Lorz A, Stein D (eds) (2009) Translation issues in language and law. Palgrave Macmillan, Basingstoke
Pérez R and R Greenwald (2004) Unprecedented: the 2000 presidential election. Greenwald Productions Films, Los Angeles
Reese LMW (ed) (1962) International contracts: choice of law and language. Columbia University, Oceana Publications, New York
Reiss K (1971) Möglichkeiten und Grenzen der Übersetzungskritik: Kategorien und Kriterien für eine sachgerechte Beurteilung von Übersetzungen. Hueber, Munich
Rossini C (1998) English as a legal language. Kluwer Law International, London
Šarčević S (1997) New approach to legal translation. Kluwer Law, Dordrecht
Strong I (2010) How to write law essays and exams. Oxford University Press, Oxford
Taylor C (1998) Language to language. A practical and theoretical guide for Italian/English translators. Cambridge University Press, Cambridge
Tiersma PM (2012) A history of the languages of law. In: Tiersma PM, Solan LM (eds) The oxford handbook of language and law. Oxford University Press, Oxford, pp 13–26
Van Rees MA (2005) Indicators of dissociation. In Eemeren van FH, Houtlosser P (eds) Argumentation in practice. John Benjamins, Amsterdam, pp 53–68
Wagner A, Cacciaguidi-Fahy S (eds) (2006) Legal language and the search for clarity. Peter Lang, Bern
Wierzbicka A (1997) Understanding cultures through their key words. Oxford University Press, New York
Williams C (2004) Legal english and plain language: an introduction. ESP Across Cultures, 11–124

Chapter 4
A Global Crime and World Hunger

The law growth of sin and doth punish it
English Proverb, 1629

4.1 Cattle Stealing: Europe and the Greek Myth

This section introduces the problem of variation in register and cultural connotation of Latin, Italian and English, related to a specific crime, i.e. cattle stealing. More specifically, the social and regional varieties of English (British, American and Australian) are compared to the Latinate term used. There are socio-cultural implications derived from cultural contexts, identity and perceptions and beliefs relating to the 'crime' and the public perception of the crime and its seriousness. Cattle stealing is interesting because it is hardly reported in the Italian press.

The crime was punished by death under Roman law. The great myths of the Mediterranean Latin and Greek world are emblematic of the 'epos' connoting the stealing of oxen, horses and heifers. Crime and punishment are infused with epos and sacred connotation. In Greek mythology, as in the *Homeric Hymns*, Hermes steals cattle of the god of the sun, Apollo. In the *Odyssey* Ulysses' companions roast the 'Oxen of the Sun' belonging to Hyperion (Helios). Such symbolism may be paired with myths about the abduction of women. The core myth of the Western world is itself a subversive paradox: a beautiful princess, Europa, is seduced and abducted (no rustling here) by a bull (Zeus/Jupiter). 'Abduction' of women and theft of livestock were practiced in many of the world's ancient cultures. There is a divine law of 'fate' for the Greek Oxen of the Sun, and American literature also has its legends and legal practices.

One recent case of literary Sardinian sheep rustling is described in a historical novel (Fois 1998). In this Italian novel, the protagonist is a *terracu*, a young servant, and he and his attorney are accused of stealing lambs. In 1848 under the 'Statuto Albertino' (Albertine Statute) of the Kingdom of Italy and Kingdom of Sardinia, which became the basis of the codification of the Italian constitution of 1861, *abigeato* was considered together with *brigantaggio* (Dezza 2011,

R. Masiola and R. Tomei, *Law, Language and Translation*,
SpringerBriefs in Law, DOI 10.1007/978-3-319-14271-5_4

pp. 422–451). Whereas in Italy *abiegato* was a way of protecting the Sardinian nobility from petty thefts, in the Wild West, Arizona and Mexican territory it had a totally different perception and iconic connotation, largely as a result of popular films, where the 'outlaw' was portrayed as a fascinating character.

Before outlining a cross-cultural comparison between *abigeato* and other English synonyms (raiding, rustling, duffing), there are some distinctive traits to note in this semantic domain. For example, the term 'kidnapping,' which today refers to people, has it etymological roots and meaning in 'sheep stealing.' A 'kid' is a lamb, the yearling of a sheep, 'the young of a goat or of a related animal such as antelope' (CED). The compound with 'knapping' refers to the verb 'to nap,' and connotes the action of stealing or snatching, as recorded in the seventeenth century. Kidnapping is a 'common law offense that overlaps with the offenses of child abduction and false imprisonment' (OLD). 'Abduction' of persons is referred to as 'taking (them) away' against their will but may also extend to animals in some cases.

4.2 Legends of the Wild West

Legendary figures include Billy the Kidd, who was also a cattle thief, and Indians as swift and dashing horse-stealers, whom Hispanics and Americans could 'legally' shoot on the spot in Southern Arizona (Otero 1998). Apache chieftains, like Geronimo and Cochise, conferred an aura of legend on the whole territory. The Apache Wars were triggered by cattle raids and stealing from the American army and by the pioneers encroaching into Apache territories. More often than not, mediation and peaceful solutions were impossible because of linguistic misunderstanding and erroneous interpretations.

There are differences in practices and objects. Italian law specifically refers to small animals, sheep and goats, a demarcation that dates back to archaic and isolated agricultural communities, such as those of Sardinian shepherds who were the vassals of their 'masters.'

American English focuses on groups of animals, such as cattle and horses presumably stampeding or running wild, supposedly branded, and cowboys and Indians have been internationally portrayed as part of the prairie in literature and by Hollywood's. Australia has its own social and penal history, and the crime has been made 'epic' in Australia's national anthem, *Waltzing Matilda* (see below). The Latin term *abigeat*, which had also been used in America (Bouvier 1850), would have seemed an unlikely charge and would not have been understood by cowboys or Indians, with the exception of Mexican raiders. American 'rustling,' African 'raiding,' Australian and New Zealand 'duffing' all have the connotation of a brave and smart action, even if in the former lynching was permitted, especially where 'swift-moving' Indians were involved. The case of Indian nations and treaties confining them to reservations is analyzed in Chap. 6.

So there is a geo-specific relevance reinforced by imagery and films featuring Texan cowboys and Indians or the '*pastorelli* or humble shepherds.' Lynching evokes an element of dread, which Latin *abigeus* does not, despite its rich background as Latinate English.

4.3 South of the Border: More Languages, More Laws

There is a difference in the perception of the words of the law regarding the same crime. The Italian Latin-derived term is loftier and more abstruse and increases the perceived harshness of the punishment. English uses a common term that is easily understood, and Anglophone nations have developed their jurisprudence and slang to define crime. Texas, the Great Plains and the Mexican border are all bilingual areas and the vastness of territories can only be managed by cattle droving and cowboys ranging and mustering horses. The Wild West, the Midwest and the Great Plains were Indian territories and areas legendary for outlaws and crime. Large-scale cattle rustling is uncommon in Europe. Films and imagery of horses, cowboys and mavericks have influenced Western thinking, and have conferred an air of lore and myth to the whole context, which reinforces the 'identity' of today's 'cattle stealers'—narcotraffickers. The modality of crime as represented in the global news and then translated is another fertile area of research (Bielsa and Bassnett 2009). This may be usefully framed and thematized using the example of animal stealing as a common global crime with its differences in punishment and media resonance.

The case of *abigeato*, in Sardinia and the south of Italy refers to sheep and goats whereas cattle stealing in the American Far West and across the Mexican-Texan border was a historical 'cowboy and Indian' crime, which has seen a recent upsurge. *Abigeato* is derived from legal Latin and is an 'inkhorn term' pertaining to a specialized lexicon the stealer would be ignorant of. The term used in Spanish is current in Mexico and is derived from Latin, *abigeato,* and is similar to the Italian. Moreover, both the terms and the crime seem to be en vogue so that in the English-Spanish dictionary, the obsolete American English *abigeat* has been revived through Mexico:

> *Abigeat*: abigeato. robo, hurto de ganado. Este delito estivo muy castigado entre los antiguos pueblos germànicos y la ley romana condeno a estos delincuentes a trabajar forzados de minas (*damnatio ad metalla*), al destierro o a muerte. (DES, Bossini and Gleener 1998).

It is also recorded in Canadian and French dictionaries, though definitions seem to differ: The French term *troupeau* is usually associated with flocks, but it can also extend to pigs and donkeys. Another definition focuses on 'ten sheep or ten goats.' The respective uses are taken from Jean-Paul Doucet's *Dictionnaire de Droit Criminel* (2014). Historical definitions differ in time and place, and feature significant variations in the perceived offense, e.g. ten sheep, would mean the death penalty under the Customary of Bretagne. The last definition on *brigands siciliens* addicted to this crime from times immemorial is emblematic of the difficult relations in the Mediterranean area. Reference is made to French authoritative literature, specifically quoting authors and their works:

> L'abigeat s'analyse en un vol aggravé, qui consiste à détourner un troupeau appartenant à autrui en vue d'en disposer ou de se l'approprier. Il était spécialement incriminé en droit romain et dans notre Ancien droit.
> Jousse (*Traité de la justice criminelle*): On appelle abigeat, le crime de ceux qui détournent et emmènent les troupeaux, soit de bœufs, vaches, moutons, cochons, chevaux, ânes, ou autres, des endroits où ils paissent, pour se les approprier.
> Brillon (*Dictionnaire des arrêts du Parlement*): Le crime d'abigeat est de détourner ou dérober un troupeau, comme de dix brebis ou de dix chèvres ... la peine en est arbitraire en France.
> Saint-Edme (*Dictionnaire de la pénalité*): L'art. 627 de la coutume de Bretagne porte que ceux qui volent des chevaux, des boeufs ou d'autres bêtes de service et de labour, doivent être punis de mort ... Dans l'usage on condamnait ordinairement aux galères.
> Tarde (*La philosophie pénale*): *Une bande de brigands siciliens pratique de temps* immémorial les mêmes procédés ... abigeato (vol de gros bétail dans les champs) (DDC 2014, emphasis added).

More precisely, the term derives from the legal Latin: *abigeātus,* → *abigeus*, 'cattle thief' from the Latin verb. Abigo → ab + ago: drive away, from which the rarely used English 'abactor' comes.

> *Abactor*: abigeatore; l'abigeato è detto più spesso cattle stealing; costituisce una forma di theft (FDG 1984, p. 275).

In other legal dictionaries curiously enough, the term is unrecorded (West 2009), not even entered as 'cattle stealing.' The syntagm is equally absent in non-specialized dictionaries, whereas the verb 'to rustle' in its extended meaning is entered as used chiefly in the US and Canada to mean stealing horses or cattle. A 'rustler' is a cattle or horse thief (CED 2000, p. 1349). The prevailing North American usage and connotative meaning of the term is the sound of low whispering or rubbing sound as of leaves, and has been extended to the swift movements of native Indians when stealing horses.

Under Italian law it refers to theft of three or more animals from the herd or flock, and cattle or horses not from the herd. Until 1999, the Criminal Code punished *abigeato* as a form of aggravated theft. With the assumption of aggravation, the law was intended to provide protection for livestock and the agricultural economy. In view of its lack of social relevance in Italy today, the crime was decriminalized (25 June 1999, n. 205 and by the decree of 30 December 1999, no. 507) The Italian scenario of *abigeato* and its 'lack of social relevance' is totally different than 'cattle stealing,' for example in Texas, and the upsurge of cattle stealing in drug wars across the border with Mexico. In the following section, the location of the crime and its socio-cultural impact will be further expanded, and it will analyze differences within the post-colonial Anglophone world and the current resurgence of what, in Europe, was until recently considered a thing of the medieval past. In terms of the translation of common-law derived systems versus Roman law, this challenges theoretical and methodological issues previously restricted to European cases. The media now covers cases in Hispanic countries such as Mexico

(Araguàs et al. 2011). There is an increasing interest in this specific domain of law and translation in non-European countries, especially in countries and regions like Canada, Hong Kong, and the Mexican border. The field of bilingual areas, which was largely unexplored in the early decades of modern translation studies, has received unprecedented attention since the nineties and the new millennium, when English became an international legal language, from Mexico to Japan (e.g., Didier 1990; Cao 2007; Alcaraz and Hughes 2014; Goodman 2012; Fuji 2013). The following sections feature a thematized case-study, namely cattle stealing as reported in the media and national laws in postcolonial countries like Australia, New Zealand, India, South Africa and the Americas. The following sections concentrate only on aspects of language and web-mediated communication. From a linguistic point of view, there are several terms that pertain to English varieties or legal English, which have no direct 'one-word' symmetrical equivalent in other languages. For example 'larceny' is a term that frequently occurs in bills and provisions regarding cattle stealing (in Australia and New Zealand, but not in the UK). It has specific pre-modifiers (compound larceny, grand larceny, etc.), as seen in previous chapters. In American English (WLDC) 'larceny' is premodified by the term 'Felonius,' which is no longer used in British legal English: "*Felonious* stealing, taking and carrying, leading, riding, or driving away another's personal property with the intent to convert it or deprive the owner thereof." Spanish, Italian and French have one generic term 'robo/vol/furto.' In German, *Diebstahl.*

4.3.1 Messing with Texas: Rustling and Ranching

There is a dramatic resurgence of the crime in all its renewed magnitude and ferocity, as in Mexico and borderland areas it is run by narcotraffickers. Levels of cattle raiding peaked in 2010. This excerpt is from the article 'Ranching No Man's Land' on the Texas borderland area:

> Mexico has belatedly discovered that its criminal syndicates have become so powerful that they directly threaten the state. In fact, Mexico hovers on the brink of becoming a narco-state. Its criminal syndicates control the Mexican side of the Texas/Mexico border and the smuggling of drugs and illegal immigrants into Texas. Their influence and reach have crossed the Rio Grande River in ways that many politicians and media prefer to not acknowledge.[1]
>
> Caught in this crossfire are ranchers trying to protect their property and their way of life. Here are some of the problems they face daily. To understand the security problem along the Texas/Mexico border, you must understand the criminal organizations that control it.

[1] Reference is from West's (WLCD) multilingual dictionary. It is omitted in other English-Italian dictionaries, a rather common practice when there be no one-to-one equivalent.

> The drug cartels are the top tier of organized crime on the border. Alliances and territories change, but the primary cartels operating along the Texas border include the Gulf, Sinaloa, Juárez, Beltrán-Leyva, Los Zetas, Los Negros and La Familia gangs.[2]

There is nothing remotely heroic in this compared to tales of Indian resistance to reservations and Geronimo's offer to endure the constraints of forced immobility in a constricted space as a cattle rancher. Theft is on the rise despite tougher penalties, and it is not a hunger crime committed by the disinherited of the earth, nor one that excites any kind of social understanding. The term 'felony' occurs here in Mason County (Austin) report:

> Thieves who steal cattle will face harsher penalties starting last week. Persons who steal less than 10 head of cattle, horses, exotic wildlife or fowl could be convicted of a third degree felony and face up to 10 years in prison, according to a law passed by the Texas Legislature in May that went into effect last Tuesday.[3]

The Web offers free access to anyone, and inventive citation is the rule, yet this blog demonstrates a particularly emotional reaction:

> Comment: I was recently told by an acquaintance with some knowledge of Texas law (I live in Austin), that anti-horse thief laws are still on the books, such that *stealing horses is to this day punishable by death* by *hanging in the state of Texas.* Not that I plan on stealing any horses, lol! The interesting 'twist' to it, is that this acquaintance said that it is legal in Texas in the case of horse theft, for people to make 'citizen's arrests' with respect to horse thieves, and even carry out the penalty themselves.[4]

Cattle rustling, as it is commonly referred to in the US, was a crime that in Texas was punished by death. There is a flurry of blogging on the question of whether cattle rustling is still a hanging offense in the US or any other nation. This can only widen the cultural and juridical distance gap between Europe and the U.S.

4.4 Duffing Down-Under: Australia and New Zealand

'Duff' is a word with many different meanings, idiomatic, slang, dialectal and metaphorical. From the metaphor of 'dough' it denotes a raisin cake; in Northern dialects it connotes something stale, it also means to fake and deceive, to misrepresent or to have a deceptive appearance. It would later shift from slang to a technical term in golf. In British usage it means to misplay or misjudge one's swing so that the club strikes the ground behind the ball before hitting it. As a noun a 'duffer' can informally refer to an incompetent person. In dialect forms it is a peddler or a hawker. In Australian English 'to duff' denotes the crime of stealing

2 http://www.thecattlemanmagazine.com/archives/2010/12/no-man's-land.html. David Crosby. 'Ranching Wild Texas' was from January 2010 Issue. Access 9 November 2014.

3 http://stateimpact.npr.org/texas/2013/08/20/cattle-theft-on-the-rise-in-texas-despite-tougher-penalties/. Mose Buchele. August 20, 2013. Access November 9, 2014.

4 http://message.snopes.com/showthread.php?t=40357. December 28, 2008.

cattle and/or to alter the brand on stolen cattle. Recorded usage in this sense dates back to the nineteenth century.[5]

Cattle raiding, or *cattle duffing* as it is called in Australia and New Zealand, seemed to be a thing of the distant past, with legendary protagonists featured in the first novels of Australian literature, such as the notorious Captain Starlight in Rolf Boldrewood's *Robbery Under Arms* (1888), which stood for Australia's wild freedom in the spirit in the bush and 'private initiatives' targeted at wealthy pastoralists and their sheep stations. New laws passed, indicate that the crime, which appeared to have declined, is back and duffers are striking again in the face of world depression and famine.

Reactions are not as desperate as in Jamaica (machete), or famine-torn South Sudan where blood-compensation is demanded. Still, penalties are increasing and more people are taking risks and suffering as a result of this global crisis. Australia is a Federation of States, and not all states have the same agricultural and productive features. Queensland is traditionally a territory rich in sugar-cane plantations, mining and farming (and stunning beaches). Though a wealthy state, it still reports a high rate of duffing. In recent years, the Criminal Law Amendment Bill has been passed on 'stock theft' and there is also a 'Stock Squad.' From the title or taken out of context, one could infer that the crimes involve stock exchange dealings.

> The Criminal Law Amendment Bill 2002 (Qld) contains provisions that increase the maximum penalties for *livestock theft* and related offences. The increases will result in Queensland having some of the strongest penalties for *livestock offences* in Australia. Queensland and Western Australia are the only two States that maintain a dedicated stock investigation squad, as the other States have absorbed *stock investigation* work into general policing (Queensland Parliamentary Library 2002/2008)

In this dedicated survey, the Parliamentary Library of the State of Queensland gives data, historical facts and long-term statistics on livestock and crime, and compares them with other agricultural Australian States. There are sections devoted to 'Circumstances of Aggravation' (in Italy this has been eliminated), Community Expectations of Increased Penalties, Historical Overview and the Extent of Rural Crime.[6] What emerges is a technical upgrading in the way crimes are committed; helicopters and other technical equipment are used for a crime, which in Queensland alone results in losses of 2 million Australian dollars. It is far removed from the days of nostalgic duffing. As prices for herds increase, the proceeds from stock theft also increase, making it a lucrative venture, which is on the rise. The 'Stock Squad' of today definitely has more appeal than old-time duffers. Laws and the structure of 'stock theft' differ within communities and nationwide. These theft provisions from some ten years ago refer to Queensland (Australia) and were the result of the judiciary being criticized for failing to hand out penalties sufficiently harsh to deter

---

[5] In slang it also denotes the rump or buttocks (CED). In Australian Slang it is also a mine that proves unproductive.

[6] In the Italian Code aggravation has been eliminated.

would-be offenders. Theft encompasses farm machinery, and equipment, not only animals.

> The use of motorcycles, portable yards, trained dogs, livestock transporters and even helicopters in remote areas are measures of the arsenal available to contemporary livestock thieves, but policing is not far behind with access to global positioning systems, laptop computers, video cameras and satellite telephones. (2008, p. 1)

Australian state legislature has historically taken stock theft seriously. In 1865, the Queensland parliament passed the first piece of legislation, the Larceny Act. It provided for a maximum of fourteen years imprisonment for the offense of stealing cattle (steers, bulls, bullocks etc.). Compared to British legislation, the respective terms are still commonly used. Fourteen years is a very harsh punishment, and there were also monetary penalties for cases of suspected crimes. Those viewed as professional thieves were to be treated differently to individuals who steal for food. The story narrated in Australia's national anthem *Waltzing Matilda* featuring 'a jolly swagman' and a *jumbuck* (sheep) epitomizes popular lore. 'Captain Starlight' portrayed in the cited novel is yet another hero from the colorful stories of cattle duffing and bushranging.

Henry Redford (1841–1901), also known as 'Captain Starlight,' was a famous cattle drover and a notorious duffer. When he faced trial, the jury was so impressed by his achievements as a tracker, drover and explorer that they found him not guilty! 'The man and the myth' is still popular in Australian cultural memory and with the media. An annual three-week Redford Cattle Drive commemorates his exploits as a drover.

Duffing is an Australian word, and New Zealand cannot boast legendary *cattle duffers*, as its traditional pastoralism is based on sheep, and its grazing territory is not as vast as the continent of Australia. However, James Mackenzie is New Zealand's answer to Captain Starlight. Online media reports feature recent cases of *rustling* (American English), which is preferred to the Australian term. Sheep are New Zealand's staple product, as reflected in the online article 'Lost Sleep'

> There exists a romantic notion of the outlaw rustler – a lone man and his dog under a moonlit sky. Sheep rustling sounds like one of the most ancient and quaint. We even named a beautiful part of our country after one; the Mackenzie Country in South Canterbury takes its name from James Mackenzie, a Scottish shepherd-tuned-rustler, who was caught driving 1000 sheep through the basin in 1855.
> These days, Kiwis must cop his or her fair share of sheep jokes, but as any farmer who has been robbed of their flock will tell you, it is no laughing matter. In fact, one Rotorua farmer who had been hit by stock thieves six times in a year said it could result in homicide, knowing his rustlers used firearms that had left his sheep 'running around with bullet holes.[7]

The context is not as violent as Texas calling for the death penalty when faced with narcos and with cattle theft and drug trafficking beginning to merge. There are

[7] http://www.stuff.co.nz/the-press/news/9981215/Stock-rustling-costing-up-to-120m-a-year. April 20, 2014. Access April 23, 2014.

also differences compared to Australia's reactions. In New Zealand innovative measures to fight crimes include the use of drones, and DNA testing for stolen animals. Perception of the crime is also different: 'Stock theft, or rustling in New Zealand falls into two categories: chancers who grab one or more animals from a herd for their freezer, and those who drive a more substantial number from the farm' (Ibid.). Meat is sold on the black market and the crime of rustling is classed as 'general theft.' Curiously, the charge comes under the Animal Products Act, and selling meat on the black market can be punished by up to two years in prison and a fine of up to NZ $100,000.

4.5 Africa and Jamaica: Blood Compensation and Machetes

Now, from peaceful New Zealand farmers let's move on to Afro-Caribbean and African communities. In Jamaica animal theft is traditionally a type of one-animal theft, motivated by hunger. More recently it has been committed by roving bands of thieves stealing cattle and horses. In October 2013 (last year), a man caught stealing was hacked to death. The online edition of *The Jamaica Observer* reported the incident using terms like 'praedial larceny':

> Twinley Jones, 34, a higgler of Moores district in Rock Rover, Clarendon was Wednesday chopped to death by a mob in Lucky Valley district, also in the parish. Jones and other two men were accused of stealing cows in the Ward Hill district…Residents confronted the men and this escalated into an argument which resulted in Jones being chopped several times… Up to Monday this week, there were a total of 231 reported cases of praedial larceny…

There is a blend of law language, *praedial larceny*, and the Jamaicanism *higgler*. A higgler is an itinerant dealer, a huckster, 'formerly an itinerant peddler, now also one who brings produce into a market to sell' (DJE). Both terms are obsolete in British language usage. Newspaper comments posted highlight the emotional attitude to justice (either justifying the vigilantes' machete or condemning it). The term 'crooks' is here applied to 'thieves.' These are two random posts:

> Nuff (enough) animal *crooks* in this parish. Not the first times for vigilante justice happening here like everywhere … (Mars)

> I can't condone a *mob killing* in any society. But I don't feel sorry for the victim. How terrible is it for the poor farmer trying to make a living only to have his livestock stolen, taking food and other necessities from his family… (jamdel51).

Farmers with machetes ward off thieves from property, yet violence caused by cattle-theft is peaking. The Jamaican higgler, however, did not carry arms. Jamaica calls this 'jungle justice' and perceives it as mob warfare, Africa is calling for other measures. Sudan demands 'blood compensation' and forceful disarmament. The crime is spreading across African states, from South Africa to South Sudan. The period referred to in the media is the same as in Jamaica (summer-fall 2013).

The growing number of sophisticated violent 'cattle raids' are a threat to the stability according to a UN Mission in South Sudan. The use of guns and weapons in cattle raiding has the power to destabilize the country, in view of the large area and magnitude of livestock farming. It is not a matter of neighbors, crooks, gangs or mobs, but of tribal clash after two decades of civil war. The UN Mission report came after hundreds of people lost their lives in cattle raids in Jonglei State (25,000 heads stolen). The term used in the press is 'rustling' and 'raiding':

> Awash with arms, over two decades of civil war, South Sudan still suffers from communal rivalry. Local governments in South Sudan have begun enforcing forceful disarmament to eliminate *cattle rustling* and clashes between communities. Officials in the East African country have long decried *armed cattle rustling*, which has often caused bloody tribal clashes among communities. Awash with arms, after over two decades of civil war, South Sudan still suffers from communal rivalry. 'The initiative is aimed at restoring peace and security in the state that has been affected by cattle raids. At any time we will stage a forceful disarmament, we will deploy a large number of security force at county and village levels to carry out the exercise,' said Unity State Security Advisor, Manyiew Dak.[8]

From a linguistic and criminal perspective, the use of different terms highlights the explicit and open attack of 'raids,' which appears to contradict the original American English denotation of 'rustling' as a quick, stealthy undercover action. The gravity of the situation is more indicative of civil warfare. In terms of language, the more tribal term 'blood compensation' is used instead of 'death penalty' for the punishment that will be enforced for cross-border cattle raiding. The 'Tri-state Conference on Security Issues' communiqué came only ten days after the article above. The agreement had been signed by the governors but was yet to be adopted by the three state parliaments.[9] 'Legalization of blood compensation' was the second item on the agenda, closely following 'criminalization of cattle rustling.'

The situation in South Africa is again different, from the point of view of language, law and culture, even though there are similarities. The common implication is, however, that stock theft has been steadily increasing in Jamaica, Africa (Sudan) and America, mainly in cross-border areas. In North America, in the 1860 the transition from open range to fenced grazing reduced the practice of massive raids. During the American Depression, sub-urban rustling became a new criminal practice consisting of anaesthetizing animals and taking them to auction. In the UK it is on the rise as the cost of meat increases, the targeted animals being lambs and sheep. Cattle raiding is also an issue in East Africa, for example in Northern Kenya (bordering Somalia, South Sudan and Ethiopia) where cattle raiding terrorizes civilians and kills hundreds of people. In South Africa, the Animal Identification Act (2002) completed the Stock Theft Act (1959). There is an emphasis on the duties of the owners, and marking and branding is prescribed in detail. The Police

[8] http://www.theafricareport.com/disarmament.html. Godfrey Olukya. June 7, 2013. Access June 8, 2014.

[9] http://www.sudantribune.com/spip.php?article47022. June 19, 2013. Access July 23, 2014.

Service Theft Unit has published a very detailed and specific information brochure.[10] The animals include small animals, ostriches, pigs and horses, and prevention of crime regulates slaughter, animal identification and transportation. Stock theft is a major problem as it costs the livestock industry millions of rand (430 million) every year. In South Africa there are few convictions, and legislation is perceived as lenient as it relies on identifying the animals.[11] Former governments granted land lease with options of purchase that are no longer in force and black farmer victims of theft are not all wealthy landowners.

4.6 India: Holy Cows

The conclusive section of our comparative case study on cattle stealing is emblematic of loss of traditions and identity in a world of rising hunger and crime. Increasing meat consumption has meant that holy cows are a target for unscrupulous thieves. Although these animals are mangy and scrawny, they are left to freely roam the streets, making them easy prey. In India there is another English term, which is informal and denotes shoplifting. There are people who volunteer to shelter these animals at night and receive funds from wealthy Indians for this. There is also a large shelter outside the metropolitan area where thousands of cattle live. This is a recent report from the Delhi Journal in the *New York Times*:

> Cattle rustling, called 'lifting' here, is a growing scourge in New Delhi, as increasingly affluent Indians develop a taste for meat, even the flesh of cows, which are considered sacred in Hinduism. Criminals round up some of the roughly 40,000 cattle that wander the streets of this megacity and sell them to illegal slaughterhouses located in villages not far away. …
> Many of the cattle in Delhi are part of dairy operations and their owners have neither the land nor the money to keep them penned. So the animals graze on grassy medians or ubiquitous piles of trash. Others too old to be milked are often abandoned and left to wander the streets until they die — or get picked up by the rustlers.[12]

The aim of this comparative case study was to demonstrate the dynamics that create this type of crime and the differences in language and law, as reported in the media. Not all online journals have comments posted; not all crimes display the same cruelty and violence. Some criminals have become legends of early colonial settlement (Captain Starlight and James Mackenzie); some have become symbols of native resistance to reservations (Comanche, Apache Chiricawas), and some have given up their religious tenets to globalization while others are waging a tribal feud. South America has drug wars within cattle wars; Jamaica is suffering a wave of

[10] http://www.kwanalu.co.za/upload/files/SAPSStockTheftBrochure.pdf.

[11] http://www.farmersweekly.co.za/article.aspx?id=40088&h=Developing-farmers-feel-the-scourge-of-stock-theft. Peter Mashala, May 28, 2013. Access July 23, 2014.

[12] http://www.nytimes.com/2013/05/27/world/asia/cow-thefts-on-the-rise-in-india.html Gardiner Harris, May 26, 2013. Access: June 23, 2014.

violence and social unrest and three bordering states in South Sudan are calling for blood compensation. Laws differ sharply. The language in which laws and news are reported is English. The definition of the crime and the law differ, as the English term varies in all these postcolonial areas. In Europe, notably Italy, the ancient crime of the illegal slaughter of animals and retaliation has been re-emerging with the international narco-mafia. The spread of the crime and different legal remedies are reported in English. The different English terms have no corresponding terms in European languages, should translation be needed.

References

Alcaraz E, Hughes B (2014) Legal translation explained, 2nd edn. Routledge, London
Araguàs A, Baigorri Jalòn J, Campbell H (eds) (2011) Translating the law. Theoretical and methodological issues. Comares, Granada
Bielsa E, Bassnett S (2009) Translation in global news. Routledge, London
Bouvier J (1914/1850) Bouvier's law dictionary. A concise encyclopedia of the law. Rawle's revision, vol 1. Vernon Law Book—St. Paul, Minn, West Publishing Co., Kansas City. https://archive.org/stream/bouvierslawdicti01bouv#page/n25/mode/2up 2008. Accessed 23 July 2014
Cao D (2007) Translating law. Multilingual Matters, Clevedon
Dezza E (2011) La disciplina dell'abigeato nell'età della codificazione. In: Mattone A, Simula PF (eds) [Collana Dipartimento Storia, Università di Sassari, Carrocci, Roma, 41] pp 422–451
Didier E (1990) Langue set langages du droit: étude comparative des modes d'expression de la common law et du droit civil, en français et en anglais. Wilson and Lafleur, Monreal
Fois M (1998) Sempre caro. Frassinelli – Il Maestrale, Milano
Fujii Y (2013) The translation of legal agreements and contracts from Japanese into English. Babel 59:421–444
Goodman C (2012) The rule of law in Japan. Kluwer Law International, Amsterdam
Otero MA (1998) The real billy the kid. Houston. University of Houston, Texas
West E (2009) The last Indian war: the Nez-Percé story. Oxford University Press, New York

Chapter 5
Conflicts and Clashes

Woe to you, scholars of the law!
You have taken away the key of *knowledge*.
You yourselves did not enter and you stopped those trying to enter

(Luke 11.12)

Guai a voi, dottori della legge,
che avete tolto la chiave alla *scienza*. Voi non siete entrati, e a quelli che volevano entrare l'avete impedito.

(Luke 12.4; emphasis added)

There is a substantial difference between 'knowledge' (*African Bible* based on the *New American Bible*, 2005) and 'science' (Italian *Vangelo,* official version, 2005). This conceptual difference equally affects the field of jurisprudence as defined 'science' or 'knowledge.' The tree in the Garden of Eden was the tree of 'knowledge of good and evil.'

5.1 Concepts and Crimes

This section highlights questions of power and ideology that may explain the causes and effects of unequal treaties, as a consequence of linguistic manipulation in drafting and translation. The history of the conquest of the New World involves cultural and linguistic misunderstanding, violence, genocide, slavery and dispossession of the soil. The topic of political violence and globalization is a dramatic one, its representation and resonance being mediated through translation (Bielsa and Hughes 2009). In this sense, the present approach to law and translation encompassing a range of cross-disciplinary activities and comparative studies in history, international relations, diplomacy, language, literature highlights a broader approach to law and humanities.[1] In this chapter we discuss focus and approach as

[1] See also Carpi and Ward (Carpi and Ward 2008), pp. 361–372 and Ward (Ward 1995). On the other hand there are international journals on legal communication and on semiotics and law. Chair and courses on forensic linguistics have been established in European universities (i.e., U.K. and Finland).

R. Masiola and R. Tomei, *Law, Language and Translation*,
SpringerBriefs in Law, DOI 10.1007/978-3-319-14271-5_5

the common theme of translation in contexts such as warfare, colonial expansion and declarations of war.

One basic concept of law in the Western world, derived mainly from Roman law, is that of property and property rights. Not all the peoples of the earth, however, perceive and conceptualize the sense of possession in the same way. Law is also reflected in terms of reality and space as well as the correlation and interconnections derived from the shared meaning, values and beliefs.

How can someone 'own' a territory or space that is tribal and sacred? The land is God's, and its people are part of the land in cohesive and cosmic harmony. There is no question of 'real estate,' property, ownership or nationalization here. The history of the American continent, the Westward expansion and the genocide caused by the reservation system is only one of the many episodes in history that demonstrate failures in the translation and communication of treaties. This section only focuses on some of the major factors that determined subversion in terms of natural law and equal justice.

The colonization of Australia and New Zealand is also a case of dispossession of the soil, genocidal policies and destruction of communal spaces and tribal grounds. The land-claims movement and consequent policies are yet another aspect. The most egregious wound was inflicted not on the community per se, but on those laws that were not conventionally written down in statutes according to the Western mind's systems of order. The wars between England and Spain, the ensuing wars and massacres in the New World and the slavery route are a dark side of the history of the conquest.

These tragic events developed in the context of legal instruments and imposed laws. The subsequent treaties with the Indians centuries later, the colonization of Australia, the dispossession of the soil in New Zealand, are only a few examples. In most native Amerindian cultures, the land and its people, the waters and the sky were all part of a cosmic and spiritual order. Moreover, Aboriginal languages do not categorize reality and space in terms of 'I have' 'yours' and 'mine,' and the concept of 'possession' linked to personal pronouns is not part of the language. In this context, the concept of 'I am the owner of this land' or 'this place belongs to him' is unfamiliar and disruptive to a world-order that is not based on property. There is an intricate web of cross-cultural and language issues surrounding conflicts and warfare, both between the European empires and between the Empire (i.e. Britain, Spain, France, Portugal) and its colonized natives, which calls into question 'the law' and indigenous laws against Empires.[2] One legal stereotype based on racial supremacy stated that a society that did not possess property relations and did not live within a community of laws 'could not for that reason claim ownership, possession, equity of land, soil and of what the soil contained, i.e. precious metals.' Cultural incompatibility was total, and natives had no rights. Anthony Pagden

---

[2] A collection of essays recently published (Belmessous 2011) sheds new light on the phenomenon of 'legal resistance' and the drafting of legal strategies to contest dispossession by the indigenous peoples from America, Australia and New Zealand.

supports this evidence with historical juridical arguments, as Stephen Greenblatt notes in his influential *Marvelous Possessions*:

> … the jurist Palacios Rubios had argued in 1513 that a society that did not possess property relations (and hence did not live within a legitimate civil community) could not for that reason claim on behalf of any of its individuals *dominium rerum* when confronted by invaders attempting to seize their lands. In other words, a full recognition of the profound disparity between the indigenous culture and that of the invaders would not necessarily lead *to what we regard as equity: on the contrary, it could lead to a justification for seizure* (Pagden 1987, pp. 81–92; in Greenblatt 1991, p. 169, n. 24).

So much for the justification of imperialism and conquest on doctrinal grounds. What comes to the fore in this quote, however, is that the Spanish system is not common law but is instead based on Latin or Roman law. The term ‘equity’ is alien jurisprudence based on Roman law, since ‘equity’ has been added to common law, which offers no adequate remedies, and both have been incorporated into statute law. This concluding observation focuses on the remoteness not only of the indigenous cultural systems, but also the divergence of the legal systems of Spain and England as imperial powers.

5.2 ‘Possessions’ and Colonial Conquest

As already noted, a key concept lies in the significance of the term /property/, possession and its Latin derived ‘real estate.’ The latter being based on the modifier ‘real’ which conceals a Latin etymology, based on *res-rei,* ‘the thing.’ The compounds: real action, real estate, real property, real right suggest that this is a direct reference to civil law (Italian) and the partition between:

> *diritti reali* → /real rights//rights *in rem/*in English, and
> *diritti obbligazionari, diritti di obbligazione* → obligation law, personal rights, rights *in personam*, obligation. Common law and its complement equity law coexist with ‘legal’ rights.

The case of the Spanish conquest of the New World relies on the interpretation of Latin, translated into the two different concepts of ‘possession.’ In order to understand the divergence of meaning in legal systems, contextualization and diachronic variation have to be accounted for in explaining the distinction between possession and active ‘ownership’:

> the Spanish term *tomar posesiòn* (and the Portuguese *tomar posse*) did not have the same meaning as the English ‘to take possession.’ ‘Possession’ in Elizabethan royal patents such as that granted to Sir Humphrey Gilbert and Sir Walter Raleigh means to ‘have, hold, occupy and enjoy’ and to wield over the territory so held ‘full power to dispose thereof… according to the lawes of England. (Greenblatt 1991, p. 167, n. 7)

In Spanish, the legal concept of *tomar posesiòn* referred to formulaic pronouncements and the rituals of symbolic actions, and consequently did not imply an active use and fruitful enjoyment or the exercise of ‘ownership’ rights. Elizabeth responded to Spanish complaints against Frances Drake and the 'empire' of Guyana, denying that the Spanish had 'established' possession.

> According to William Camden, the Queen denied that the Spanish had established 'possession': Spaniards, she said, 'had touched here and there upon the coasts, built cottages, and given names to a river or a cape, which does not entitle them to ownership;... Prescription without possession is worth little (Greenblatt 1991, p. 167, n. 7).

The Latin quote from the *Rerum Anglicarum* by Camden (1639, p. 328) *cum praescriptio sine possessione haud valeat* gives a clear-cut distinction. The current term 'prescription' in common law has a network of meanings and applications in the disciplines of jurisprudence and is also used in international law. Today the *querelle* implies the concept of 'positive' or 'acquisitive prescription.' The matter is subject to different regulation in civil law. The terms 'ownership' and 'property' are used in common law, and in 'property law,' ownership also extends to rights, such as ownership of 'patent' and copyrights. However, 'possession' originates from 'property' (Rose 1985). The dynamics of colonial and postcolonial cultural and legal conflicts in land claims and the extension into native territories essentially rely on diversity in concepts, values and beliefs within community practices (Belmessous 2011, 2014).

5.3 Clashes of Cultures: Signs, Symbols, Symptoms

From what we have discussed in the opening section of this chapter, it clearly emerges that the problem of understanding is not so much the terms of language and word-for-word translation, but the cultural patterns and world perception.

If the notorious 'to take possession' (Masiola Rosini 1997, pp. 174–175) were based on the meaning of the written words of the law, Roman law or common law, and Latin were still used and referred to by Spanish and English legal scholars, the case of colonial expansion and dominion would be beyond the 'legal quibbles' and word manipulation that were common practice in disputes over throne successions or rights to conquest in different European languages (Valdéon 2014).

In the case of the conquest of the New World, the clashes and irreparable damage had other origins, where the sense of spirituality and the divine were united in the figure of the emperor. The episode of the Inca Emperor and the bloodbath at Cajamarca epitomizes the clash of systems based on different ritual codes and communicative modalities.

Another example is the legal formulation of the *requerimento* or 'pronouncement,' which was read to the indigenous people as a 'declaration' that the Conquistadores had come to *tomàr posessiòn* of the new land in the name of the Spanish Crown. The *requerimento* was translated from Latin into Spanish and then retranslated. The tragedy of Cajamarca, (November 15, 1532), with the capture of Atahualpa is one of the most abominable examples of bloodshed in the conquest. The Spanish Conquistador, Francisco Pizarro was accompanied by his lieutenant

Hernan De Soto and the Dominican Fray de Valverde. There was a poorly executed attempt to explain the precepts of the Catholic religion to the Inca, an attempt that was certainly not helped by the native interpreter Felipillo. The *Comentarios Reales* written after the event by Inca Garcilaso de la Vega reports that Valverde pointed to a book saying that it contained God's words and handed it over to Atahualpa. When the Inca was presented with the book, he shook it closely to his ear and is said to have asked why the book did not speak to him. The subsequent act of smelling and licking the book was seen as an offense by the Spaniards, who were ready to attack (Masiola Rosini 1997, pp. 129–144).[3]

In translation theory and practice, this case can be contextually defined as: symbol, symptom, signal (Kelly 1979, pp. 70–88; Masiola Rosini 1988, pp. 45–49). 'Signal' aims at provoking a response in the recipient, and 'symbol' is centered on the subject matter. The question of speaking the truth in reciprocal trust, from the invader to the invaded was paramount, and this is where failure occurred.[4] If 'truth' (quality of information) and 'trust' are intentionally set aside, it will have dire effects on the whole communicative process. This may also affect international legal documents, where matters of ideology and translational issues add to the complex dynamics of cross-cultural clashes, violent conflict and the role of mediators (Inghilleri and Harding 2010, pp. 165–174; Cunico and Munday 2007, pp. 141–150).

An understanding of the differences in codes, rituals, beliefs, values and world perception would seem important considering the magnitude of violent conflict between the Western world and Islamic terrorism and fundamentalism. The cultural gaps that occur in shifting from one culture to another highlight how language affects not only international communication, but also the 'way of thinking' and what ethnolinguists generally call 'frames of mind.' David Katan in his *Translating Cultures* notes in his conclusion that he began the book by asking "what is the culture factor?" and ends by suggesting that culture is not a factor, but the framework (the context) within which all communication takes place. The mediator, translator, bilingual drafter and translating team will need to be aware of this to be able to act within the culture of the law and legal concepts:

> The cultural orientations are filters that help individuals orient themselves in society. They provide individuals with a way of interpreting the environment and guide visible behaviour that is congruent with other members of the same culture. Misperception, misinterpretation and mistranslation can easily result when these out-of-awareness orientations are not taken into consideration.
> The map individuals, as representatives of a culture, make of the world is a local map, and is not a good guide to understanding texts produced by other cultures. Hence, the heart of

---

[3] See also Todorov (1974) on Hernan Cortès, and relative exhaustive references.

[4] The reference to the question of truth and manipulation is crucial in the conquest and further colonization. This justifies the present choice of using Kelly's and Gerhard Ebeling's model correlated to deceit and lying. See also the reference to Paul Grice and 'truth' as quality factor interactions in further sections.

> the mediator's task is not to translate texts but to translate other cultures, and help strangers give new text welcome (Katan 1999, p. 241).

Legal texts are highly complex as they are subject to different and sometimes mixed juridical systems. The written text is the result of multilingual and sometimes secret negotiations for which there are no tapes or transcripts.

5.4 Ethnic Cleansing: Aborigines and the Law

The international debate on the abolition of slavery in popular and religious literature and in parliaments is also a matter of translation and cultural and linguistic contact. For more than two centuries, the slave trade went virtually unchallenged. The international abolition campaign that ultimately resulted in parliamentary acts of abolition was a slow process. Each colonial power had its own legal language and slavery terminology with definitions, categorization and a hierarchical scale of concepts institutionalized in definitions of ethnic hybridity, with a view to improving the outcome of incidental 'mixing of the races.'

Quarteroon, quinteroon, octoroon, and *Zambo* were Spanish labels based on normative standards and adapted into English and paved the way for laws related to programs of enforced racial protection of half-castes and their offspring. When it comes to the meaning of such terms and their translational equivalent, the concepts not always clear, such as the idea of *métissage* or *mestizaje* (no English here), which connotes fluidity, mutability, and ambiguity, rather than defined values of syncretism, reconciliation, unity or totality (Legrand 2005, p. 46, n. 23).[5] There were tables depicting the 'mixture of different castes under their common or distinguishing names' of over twenty different combinations, with complicated numerical fractions for South America made by the Spaniards.[6] More generally, there are several themes and legal issues that may cause legal and statutory problems, such as the communication of litigation (Beke 2014) and the understanding of passed judgment and sentences; the topic of law and language becomes a sensitive issue in postcolonial contexts.

In the case of Australia, and the topic introduced below, there may have been Reconciliation and 'compensation' to the 'stolen generation' of Aboriginal half-caste

---

[5] The author specifically refers to this concept as metaphor in law and law in translation: 'as the understanding of the rule changes, the meaning of the rule changes. And as the meaning of the rule changes, the rule itself changes. Meaning simply does not lend itself to transplantation; it is not negotiable internationally. Cross-cultural influences, rather than generate a kind of immanent rationalization across laws, lead to a local *métissage…*' (2005, p. 37).

[6] A 'Chino' (father) and a Negro (mother) give a Zambo-chino. 7/8 Negro and 1/8 Indian. W.B. Stevenson in his *Narrative of Twenty Years Residence in South America* notes that he has 'classed colours according to their appearance not according to the mixture of classes, because a child receives more colour of the father than of the mother.' (1852, p. 286; in Pratt 1992, p. 152).

children, but it was not explicitly cited as legal compensation in parliamentary address.

What happened in Australia is an example of genocidal policies and ethnic cleansing designed to achieve 'racial improvement.' The English used the Spanish words and exported them to Australia and the Aborigines. It was the legal practice of assigning the children of mixed races to the hegemonic or dominant group, under acts of the respective parliaments. Language was a priority there: native languages were strictly forbidden, and the final solution aimed at erasing the native culture and languages. This caused the loss of many languages and the disruption of the roots of many tribal communities. Implementation of this ethnic cleansing started in 1869, peaked in the 1950s and went on till the 1970s.[7] Needless to say, when the 'accusation' or 'legal remedy' was read and explained by the appointed 'protectors' to the Aboriginal community, little could be understood of its purported 'ethical' grounds for improvement and social benefit of the children.

It was only in very recent years that legal translation services and linguistic mediation were offered to native communities (Neate 2003) on the grounds that often the defendant could not understand the accusation in English, let alone the type of offense or crime committed (Eades 1992). The issue here is Anglo/Aboriginal legal translation (Cooke 1995). As reported by Justice Kriewaldt back in 1960:

> The plain fact is that in the Northern Territory of Australia, the trial of an Aborigine in most cases proceeds, and so far as I could gather, has always proceeded, as if the accused were not present. If he were physically absent, no one would notice this fact. The accused, so far as I could judge, in most cases takes no interest in the proceedings. He certainly doesn't understand that portion of evidence which is of the greatest importance in most cases, namely, the account a police constable gives of the confession made by the accused. No attempt is made to translate any of the evidence to him. If the rule requiring substantial comprehension of the proceedings was applied to the Northern Territory, many Aborigines could simply not be tried. (Kriewaldt 1960, p. 23).

Compiling a legal glossary translating legal concepts across cultures into an Australian Indigenous language is a ground-breaking project. The language is that of the Torres Island community, the community who suffered deportation. The language is a lingua franca of the Aboriginal Australians of the area. There are social reasons for this legal glossary, aimed at helping the endangered community of the post-Stolen Generation when faced with charges and sentenced to imprisonment, as noted by Lysbeth Ford and Dominic McCormack, authors of the project:

---

[7] 'The Aboriginal Protection Act of the State of Victoria dates back to *1869*. The Central Board for the Protection of Aborigines had been advocating such powers since 1860, and the passage of the Act gave the colony of Victoria a wide suite of powers over Aboriginal and 'half-caste' persons, including the forcible removal of children, especially 'at- risk' girls. By 1950, similar policies and legislation had been adopted by other states and territories.' http://en.wikipedia.org/wiki/Stolen_Generations (Access 10 October 2014). See also *Rabbit Proof Fence* film by Philip Noyce, based on the autobiography *Follow the Rabbit-Proof Fence*, by Dorris Pilkington Garimara.

> The project is a response to the statistically significant incarceration rates of Indigenous Australians, particularly in the language area considered, whose limited command or complete lack of English puts them at a severe disadvantage when they are confronted head-on by the Australian legal system.
> Magistrates, police and legal aid services regularly find themselves hamstrung by a lack of a common language to communicate with defendants, detainees and clients alike. Indigenous interpreters, while fluent in the first language of their clients, often lack sufficient and specific English competency to be able to decide the meanings of English terms. (Ford and McCormack 2005, p. 58)

What follows is one significant example of ethnic and conceptual transposition in the context of judgment and release, bail and conditional liberty. For native interpreters the term 'bail' means 'you are free to go,' as this is the last phrase the magistrate utters in the courtroom. They do not realize that it is a 'conditional liberty' requiring the defendant to return. So for BAIL the following expansion strategy has been adopted. A simplified literal English has been used, and then rephrased into Aboriginal language syntax and lexicon.

'All rights, I will just set you free today. I want you to promise me to just do these things that I will tell you. These things are:

1. You will come back here at a time that I will tell you to—that time is 4 July 2005, at 1 p.m.
2. But suppose you break these conditions, within a short time you will just return to the court and I may lock you up again'.

In cases where there is a 'suspended sentence,' the definition of when imprisonment starts is decisive. Examples may better illustrate the practice of translation as mediation in court (Ford and McCormack 2005, p. 72).[8]

'I am the magistrate and I will give you three months'
Ngay = ka pule ngay-ka nga + mpa + mut + nu
I = TOP boss big and I = TOP I will to you give = will
Merrk perrkenku + numi.
moon two + one.

With specific reference to that area and community, not until 2008 did Australian Prime Minister Kevin Rudd, at a sitting of the Parliament of Australia, present an apology to indigenous Australians as a motion to be voted on in the framework of Reconciliation policy and the centenary anniversary of the Federation of Australia (2001). Not a word in the Aboriginal language, and, no lawful compensation offered to what was a virtually genocidal policy of 'half-caste' children born within an Aboriginal community.

---

[8] The pocket glossary, under the Aboriginal title 'Those difficult words that belong to the court' was scheduled to be distributed by the Law Society of the Northern Territory (Australia) to all 500 lawyers who annually qualify to practice in the Northern Territory (Ford and McCormack 2005, p. 74).

5.5 Defining 'Genocide' and 'Democracy' in Africa

The case of Rwanda is different than the above cases in its dynamics and context, but there is a language issue here, too, since the massacre and bloodshed originated in the tribal warfare between Tootsie and Hutus. In recent years, the bleak and disquieting question of how to technically define genocide at the time of the Rwandan massacre has resounded ominously. Shunning the term 'genocide' and calling it something else ('final solution') was a way of not taking action or implementing any strong international measures during the Clinton administration. The notorious phrase 'how can you technically define genocide?' seemed to be the watchword that caused inaction on the part of President Bill Clinton and the US Ambassador to the UN, Madeleine Albright. For months (from April to May 1994), the American government debated the word 'genocide,' a crime banned by the Convention for the Prevention and the Repression of Crime and Genocide (adopted by the General Assembly of the United Nations 1948).[9]

In international law, the definition of the crime of genocide is found in Articles II and III of the 1948 'Convention on the Prevention and Punishment of Genocide.'

Article II describes two elements of the crime of genocide:

(1) the *mental element,* meaning the 'intent to destroy, in whole or in part, a national, ethnical, racial or religious group, as such,' and
(2) the *physical element* which includes five acts described in sections a, b, c, d and e. A crime must include *both elements* to be called 'genocide.'

Article III described five punishable forms of the crime of genocide: genocide; conspiracy, incitement, attempt and complicity.

Following the massacre and genocide in Rwanda in 1994, Canada and other international councils made up the International Convention on the Prevention and Punishment of the Crime on Genocide. The convention confirmed that under international law, genocide is a crime whether committed in peace or war. The convention's purpose is to prevent, suppress and punish genocide. The convention states that it includes acts intended to destroy all or parts of a national, ethnical, racial, or religious group, among the first five points: 1. Killing members of the group; 2. Causing serious bodily or mental harm to members of the group; 3. Deliberately inflicting on the group conditions of life calculated to bring about its physical destruction in whole or in part; 4. Imposing measures intended to prevent

[9] 'The nation's Security Council accepted failing their responsibility to prevent the Rwandan genocide in 1994. Council members at first acknowledged that lack of governments provided the un-political stop to the massacres and admitted many mistakes made by them in tackling this issue.' http://wikipedia.org/wiki/Role_of_the_international_community_in_the_Rwandangenocide. Access 8 October, 2014.

births within the group; 5. Forcibly transferring children of the group to another group.[10] These points are followed by reference to actions and behavior inciting genocide.

In the wake of genocidal warfare and the global spread of bloodbaths, web pages offer multilingual glossaries of the concept, listing synonyms and equivalents in the different languages and contexts. A link for the translation of the convention is available in eighty languages, with a definition of genocide and its euphemisms or coded equivalents.[11]

The German term *Endlösung,* or final solution, is historically contextualized denoting the extermination of Jews. The term 'ethnic cleansing' denotes more recent events. Tragically, such terms are used internationally, and are translated into eighty languages, although they do not have lexical symmetry. For instance, French lists a lexeme that does not exist in English: *Génocidaire*, as the active agent who perpetrates the crime.[12] The French term was used by the French media during the 1994 Rwanda massacre and was also used in the English media. German and French have many co-synonyms and metaphors, whereas Chinese, for example, lists only one word. Declarations of war, peace treaties and institutionalized propaganda rely on such keywords. From a tragic and negative perspective, such terms are context-dependent and ethnically marked in terms of linguistic and cultural hegemony.

Political studies currently highlight a communicative and translation-based approach. There has been intensive work on the transition from colonial rule or protectorate to final emancipation and the need to adopt concepts and set up constitutions and legal systems. There may be many European or other languages involved (African languages, Arabic varieties, the languages of India, China).

Frederic Schaffer in his study *Democracy in Translation* focuses on the term 'democracy.' The author approaches the topic in relation to one keyword and its contexts of usage and diachronic variation in meaning.[13] There are two coexisting terms with a variation in perceived meaning, orthography and pronunciation of the Greek-derived word 'democracy' (power of the people). An analysis of written texts revealed that the French term *démocratie,* as currently used in the press, was a close parallel to the American English usage of 'democracy.' Another example is the Wolof loan-word *demokaraasi,* which was adopted when the French colonizers were establishing the foundations of the modern Senegalese state. Like its rough

---

[10] See also https://treaties.un.org/doc/Publication/UNTS/Volume%2078/volume-78-I-1021-English.pdf. It also states.

[11] The term '*populicide*' was used in France during the 'Terreur' and the Vandée region massacre by Gracchus Babeuf, the revolutionary communist (1794).

[12] file:///C:/Documents%20and%20Settings/ThinkPad/Desktop/GENOCIDE%2080 %20LANGUAGES.htm.

[13] The approach adopted by Schaffer expounds 'conceptual analysis, the structure of concepts; how concepts get used in ordinary concepts; how specific concepts fit into a semantic field of related concepts; how the meanings of concepts evolve over time; issues that arise in translating' 1998, p. 9). Curiously the author makes no reference to Wierzbicka.

equivalents in English and French, the Wolof term can today be used to refer to electoral institutions and multipartism. All three concepts, in short, have similar institutional referents. The main question, however, is whether they also share ideals or standards (Schaffer 1998, p. 19). The context is of many post-colonial nations, with the language of the colonizers and conceptualization of key terms when it came to setting up a judicial system, laws and a constitution that is drafted and available in the different languages (e.g., Sudan, South Africa).

Language and culture is what makes the difference. The next section focuses on ethics, culture and ideology in translation. Moral conflicts and real conflicts are part of the dynamics of legal reasoning (Veitch 1999) overlapping with legal adaptation and advocacy to translational ethics

5.6 Translation: Ethics, Culture and Ideology

Different channels are used for translation in the form of bilingually drafted memorandums and agreements on the one hand, and for the translation of the negotiations that precede them on the other. Negotiations, concessions and denials take place within a bargaining zone of mutual consent. The dialogue and the verbal phase of discussions and the minutes and drafts are private and confidential and remain undisclosed but are, however, the basis for the final written treaty.

Legal and peacekeeping negotiations in a range of situations in violent conflicts (Bielsa and Hughes 2009) and the codes and rituals of diplomacy raise several questions such as those of ethics, law and neutrality. These factors all impact on statutory interpretation and translation (Bennion 2002). In her introduction to *Nation, Language and the Ethics of Translation*, Sandra Bermann recognizes the role of translation in international law and politics in terms of 'translationality':

> The global reach of international law and politics only heightens the importance of language and translation. Military networks, governmental agencies, as well as international entities such as the United Nations, the United Arab Emirates, and the European Union translate for purposes of intelligence, negotiation, and the dissemination of information or propaganda, as do the growing number of nongovernmental (NGOs) agencies, be they religious or secular (Bermann and Wood 2005, p. 2)

Another aspect is that of legal issues, globalization and situations where the role of cultural as well as linguistic entities and communities is 'only beginning to be theorized.'

> They tend to raise questions about linguistic power and the dissemination of texts in various media; they bring to the fore issues of human rights as well as intellectual property; they also illuminate disparities among states, nations and local traditions, and the often tragic problems of linguistic and cultural diasporas; they reveal complex multiplicities in the shadow of apparent unity (Bermann and Wood 2005, p. 2).

Following Katan's previously noted advocacy of cultural awareness, there are also observations on the dangers of 'culture-centric' practices in light of constant wars. There is an additional comment on interpreters in warfare:

> Given the likelihood that 'culture-centric' information warfare will continue to be a strategy of the US military in fighting terrorism, interpreters will continue to play an increasingly prominent role across the globe as cultural brokers and informants, and to have an influence over how a conflict unfolds (Inghilleri 2010, p. 193).

This makes the case for objective and fair information and ethics in mediation. Austin's cooperative principle and shared principle of cooperation for 'felicity conditions' in interaction (1962), and Grice's (1975) maxims of quantity, quality, relevance, and manner seem to be the perfect way to correlate bilateral legislature and bilingual drafting. In terms of quality, it refers to truthfulness and good evidence.

Declarations of war in translation are symbolic of how 'quality' can be totally distorted and manipulated. A case in point is Japan's declaration of war on the United States and the reference to the difference in time zones in the vast area of the Pacific preceding the attack on December 8, 1941. There are other noteworthy cases in 'diplomacy' and official documents, where determination to abide by absolute truth is at stake and translation of legal terms is paramount to war or peace in the contemporary era, from the atomic bomb on Hiroshima, August 1945 to UN Resolutions, as noted by Peter Newmark:

> Its importance is highlighted by the mistranslation of the Japanese telegram sent to Washington just before the bomb was dropped on Hiroshima, when *mokasutu* was allegedly translated as 'ignored' instead of 'considered,' and the ambiguity in UN Resolution 242, where 'the withdrawal from occupied territories' was translated as *le retrait des territoires occupés*, and therefore as a reference to all of the occupied territory to be evacuated by the Israelis (Newmark 1988, p. 7)

Once more we are confronted with ambiguity in performance and translation. Whether this is due to polysemy and semantic constraints, legal quibbles and loopholes, or just a translator's mistake is a moot point. Legal translating, whether multilateral or bilateral, is done in teams and under multilingual supervision. What is 'unilateral' is the interpretation of translation, which may differ from the original text and its translation.

Polysemy, vagueness in lexical units, ambiguity, lexical asymmetry, false Latinate friends and the absence of a legal institution in the target legal system are not uncommon problems in translating legal documents and practice. Texts illustrating translation practices feature such items from different systems (Alcaraz and Hughes 2014).

A state of mutual trust, freedom from prejudice and ideological constraints is another factor in preventing distortions or manipulation of treaties. Ideology is essentially one conditioning factor in interpretation, which affects translation. To be more precise, an original text is 'interpreted' and its multilingual translation is re-interpreted. In this sense there is 'one linguistic translation' and 'two' conceptual interpretations ascribing meaning in terms of agreement, disagreement and contest. Not surprisingly, Pierre Legrand's 'Issues in the Translatability of Law' challenges the possibility of crossing boundaries and of 'transplantation' of rules that are conceptualized and embedded as culture-specific:

> Lawyers must adopt a view of law as a polysemic signifier, which connotes *inter alia* traditionary (sic) and cultural referents. If one agrees that, in significant ways, a rule receives

> its meaning from without, and if one accepts that such ascription of meaning by an interpretative community effectively partakes in the ruleness of the rule—indeed, in the *nucleus* of ruleness—it must follow that there could only occur a meaningful 'legal transplant' when both the propositional statement as such *and* its ascribed meaning—which jointly constitute *the rule* —are transported from one legal culture to another (Legrand 2005, p. 36).

The history of mankind is based on legal quibbles and a sense of entitlement to 'rightful' interpretations conditioned by ideological factors, and on political engagement contributing to geopolitical shifts, for better or worse. As such, any study of translation and ideology will inevitably rely on power and cultural issues.

More than three decades ago, in the wake of Nida's approach to Bible translation for oral cultures, the focus of the dynamics of cultural contacts initiated a major new phase in translation studies. This was not simply focused on lexical symmetry or based on 'one author' and one literary work, usually a poem, but on the primacy of context and culture. One of the most debated issues is that of cultural features and their role and influence in translational praxis.

What follows is a passing reference to those who paved the way in the seventies to highlighting translation theory and practice as pivotal to culture and cultural systems. It was a challenging new approach downgrading prescriptive norms and limits of merely 'operative' principles of manuals based on word units, usually in fixed language-pairs, e.g. French and English. The trend highlighted the context of authentic texts and their 'original' translations. This underlines the importance of an awareness and knowledge of different cultures, representing a *conditio sine qua non* for international legal contexts. The balance between what is, what seems, and what can be partially translated in the rise of translation studies also indirectly compensated for the lack of available resources for the legal translator and mediator. There are words and expressions that are peculiar to a specific legal culture, and as in the case of English and many other civil law systems, Latin is the language of such concepts and expressions. Common law uses Latin expressions, either due to tradition or as loan expressions: on the surface, this would seem to imply that the term is untranslatable and should be left in Latin. However, this is not the case: sometimes the term is embedded in legal discourse and may coexist with a semantic equivalent. This is what shapes the culture and language of a legal system. Cross-cultural translation means sharing the same mental models within a system of congruent and interrelated beliefs, values, strategies and cognitive environments (Katan 1999).

5.7 Transactions and Diplomacy: China and Hong Kong

One of the aim of this section of the book is to analyze how language and culture can act as filters and cause changes in meaning when we are confronted with 'real' meaning and extended 'metaphorical' meanings, or failed interpretation of metaphor in the making of war and the building of peace: the implications are that if violence and war break out, there should be no misunderstanding in drafting, preparing and (re)constructing the culture of peace. Definitions and conflicting interpretations of semantic (literal) meaning, as opposed to pragmatic (dynamic) meaning in situational context, represent intrinsic elements of international practice in the written judicial instruments. They may contribute to tensions arising through different 'perceptions,' misconstructions or contentious issues. As noted, the primary language source of the legal system, and the related translational issues can represent obstacles and filters in the process of international relations and communication.

Language and words, their meanings, and more often their contentious definition, have often played a fundamental role in the preliminary causes of war and final ultimatums involving diplomatic translation or mistranslation. Western history has developed on the basis of the interpretation of linguistic ambiguities in bilingual or multilingual translations for declarations of war, conscription, peace treaties, memoranda, agreements and resolutions. In many cases related to colonial conquest treaties and conventions, agreements were transplanted from oral sources or sign systems, and then from the colonizers' language back into the natives' linguistic systems. Needless to say, there was a loss in terms of legal concepts and meanings during this interpretative and drafting process. In some cases the native mediator was painfully alienated from the trust of his tribal community. In the New World, interpreters and mediators functioned as conduits through which information flowed between worlds in collision, translating more than just words and bringing comprehensibility to otherwise meaningless states' (Karttunen 1994, p. xi).

In the current scenario of constant warfare or military intervention, communication, linguistic rights and international resolutions essentially rely on international bodies for the enforcement of rulings. Guidelines and resolutions, in fact, depend on the work of translation teams, which represent 'silent partners' in the whole diplomatic process and evolution of negotiations' (Menghesha 2008).[14] The war of words and their ascribed meanings have triggered constant claims and complaints and subsequent calls for revisions. A literal interpretation may lead to incomprehension or endless legal wrangling within the domain of both international law and linguistic hermeneutics, and sometimes there may be cultural remoteness and diverging systems.

As 1997, the year of the Hong Kong handover, drew near, the concern for bilingual drafting and legal translation of remote cultures produced interesting pioneering studies assessing the quality of legal translation in the two legal systems (Mok 1995, pp. 193–208). Interesting surveys followed suit in the wake of China's upturn in translation studies interfacing with Western perspectives on the same issues (Cao 2004; Yang 2008, 2012).

[14] At the FIT (Federation of Interpreters and Translators) World Congress in Shanghai 2008 Johannes Menghesha, who was responsible for communication services at the UN, delivered his speech to an audience of thousands. The participants included high-ranking Chinese ministers, many of which had worked as diplomats and translators on international treaties.

A deep cultural divide between China and Great Britain is bluntly asserted by Qiànlòng, Emperor of the Celestial Empire, in a letter sent to King George III concerning the proposals of the British Ambassador. He states that there is no room for the spread of a new religion, and there are differences, which should be respected:

> Supposing that your Envoy should come to our court, his language and national dress differ from that of our people, and there would be no place in which to bestow him. It might be suggested that he might imitate the Europeans permanently residing in Peking and adopt the dress and customs of China, but it has never been our dynasty's wish to enforce people to do things unseemly and inconvenient. Besides, supposing I sent an Ambassador to reside in your country, how could you make for him the requisite arrangements? Europe consists of many other nations besides your own: if each and all demanded to be represented at our court, how could we possibly consent? This thing is utterly impracticable. How can our dynasty alter its whole procedure and system of etiquette, established for more than a century, in order to meet your individual views? (in Backhouse and Bland 1941, pp. 322–331).

And again what follows in this translation is overt and explicit:

> If you assert that your reverence for Our Celestial Dynasty fills you with a desire to acquire our civilization, our ceremonies and code of laws differ so completely from your own that, even if your Envoy were able to acquire the rudiments of our civilization, you could not possibly transplant our manners and customs to your alien soil. Therefore, however adept the Envoy might become, nothing could be gained thereby (ibid.).

The question of the Treaty of Hong Kong came to the fore when expiry of the mandate (1997) was drawing near. It raised comments on the metaphorical meaning of 'ninety years' which could have stood for a 'very long time,' or as the law requires, for a precise time reference. The Treaty followed opium wars, the treaty of Nanking and ultimately the extortion of New Territories for 99 years.

The question also focused on the term and concept of 'lease' clarifying the notion of 'public international lease' virtually alien to the Chinese system. Other terms involved in the revisions of the treaty were those of 'sovereignty,' 'expropriation' and 'reversionary property.' There were missives and mandates, memorandums on delimitations, notices and the 'Proclamation for the application of Hong Kong Laws on the New Territories.' Such official documents started with elaborate introductory paragraphs. As diplomatic tension mounted in the first phase, at the time of Lord Palmerston, the language was offensively explicit: in one missive Lord Napier is referred to as a 'lawless slave, a dog barbarian, an outside savage'.[15]

---

[15] Lord Napier artfully circulated propaganda against the Canton officials. This is the reaction by Governor Lu in August 1834: "A lawless foreign slave, Napier, has issued a notice. We know not how such a dog barbarian of an outside nation as you, can have the audacious presumption to call yourself Superintendent (of Trade). Being an outside savage Superintendent, and a person in an official situation, *you should have some little knowledge of property and law*. You have passed over ten thousand miles in order to seek a livelihood; you have come to our Celestial Empire to trade and control affairs—*how can you not obey well the regulations of the Empire?* You audaciously presume to break through the barriers [i.e. entrance to the city of Canton forbidden to foreigners]...According to the laws of the nation, the Royal Warrant should be *respectfully requested to behead you; and openly expose your head to the multitude*, as a terror to perverse

The last sentence of the 'special notice' to proclamation had a rather different connotation. The concept of 'lease' was translated from English into Chinese and back again and was defined within the terms 'boundary' and 'territory,' which in the history of occupation have always been key terms in disputes.[16] The context referred to the Proclamation issued by the San On district magistrate and viceroy of Canton regarding the New Territories, March 1899. There is reference to the graves, and here one must bear in mind the spiritual link with the beliefs and values inherent the cult of family ancestors. A special status of boundary and delimitation refers to the intricate network of rivers and streams in the New Territories, which were needed to convey goods and to delimiting the Kowloon Extension, where the mountain path should be the boundary:

> All waterways and roads are included within the leased area but are always to be open to the use of the people of both nations.
> Your inhabitants are hereby notified that within the leased area as delimited all fields, lands, houses, graves, local customs, and usages will remain unchanged. You need not, therefore, be alarmed or suspicious and you must be careful not to create trouble. Those villages not included in the leased territory will continue to be within Chinese territory and the people living in them are not in any way concerned.
> Should any one dare to avail themselves of pretexts to excite or mislead the minds of the people with a view to create trouble, they will most certainly be punished without leniency.[17]

As it happened, with the 1997 handover of Hong Kong from Britain to China, the new system required new drafting. It has been argued that people are in general proud of their common law-based legal systems; they are uneasy, however, with the imported English terms. The work of translating 400 statutes into Chinese was not an easy task.

> Before the handover in July 1997 when legislation began to be drafted and enacted in both English and Chinese, the Chinese version of the Hong Kong law, which carries equal legal force, was essentially prepared through translation from the English law. This is despite the fact that the Department of Justice does not deem it to be so (Law Drafting Division of Department of Justice 2001, p. 2). As such, it naturally carries with it all the problems related to the comprehension of the source language, transfer of the message, and expression in another language that attend any translation: misinterpretation, misrepresentation, and so-called 'translationese,' that is, translated text has been so influenced by the grammar of its original language that it contains awkward and unnatural expressions from the literal translation and can be easily defined as a translation. To solve these problems, the three principles of 'accurate meaning,' 'similar form' and 'good Chinese' have been formulated for the Hong Kong law (Chan 2002, p. 128).[18]

(Footnote 15 continued)
dispositions. (Iannelli 2006: xxiv; emphasis added). The reference to 90 years in the treaty implied cession in perpetuity.

[16] Free Territory of Trieste, under the Allied Military Government occupation, after ww2.

[17] The translation is by J.H. Stewart Lockhart, Colonial Secretary. Published in *The Hong Kong Government Gazette*, 1899, p. 1559.

[18] Chan refers to Emily Wai-yee Poon's observations made 10 years before (2002, p. 76).

Today Hong Kong has a new bilingual jurisdiction. Deborah Cao, in her in-depth survey on *Translating Law,* observers:

> Hong Kong courts in recent years have dealt with issues arising from bilingual legislation in a limited number of cases where 'ordinary rules' of statutory interpretation apply to bilingual laws. Such ordinary interpretative rules include the literal rule, the golden rule and the purposive or mischief approach and many others used in the Common Law jurisdictions (Cao 2007, p. 128)

It is worthwhile noting that recent approaches to Chinese translation studies and law studies emphasize the concept of harmony. Harmony is a basic tenet of Chinese poetry, Chinese traditional beliefs and values, and can be seen in their recent approach to formulating laws and diplomatic translation (Xu 2000; Xie 2010; Yang 2008). It has also been asserted as a principle in establishing relations with distant cultures and different political and legal systems. Diplomatic translation is hence seen as a sensitive issue as it may bridge or distort respectful communication. The idea of respectfulness and modesty is expressed in the ideological connotation of the *Tao Guang Yang Hui,* literally 'maintaining a low profile.' In 2008 the Chinese government published a white paper titled *China's Efforts and Achievements in Promoting the Rule of Law.* This publication received international recognition as noted by Yang Minxing in the study on 'principles and tactics on diplomatic translation':

> (it)… greatly cleared up the misunderstanding of the Chinese rule of law on the part of the Western countries. Most importantly, the relevant department paid adequate attention to the objective and just languages easily acceptable to the international community and also tried their utmost to avoid sententious political discourses in the course of drafting and translation thereof. At present, the international public opinion is a discourse system overwhelmingly dominated by the Western countries, particularly the U.S. It is necessary to have a thorough understanding of *Tao Guang Yang Hui* against the then Chinese cultural background and also to take into account the acceptability and the likely response of the audience in the Western context, so as to avoid the unnecessary misunderstanding and suspicion resulting from the difference in cultural values between China and the Western countries (Mingxing 2012, p. 9).

The recent events (October 2014) and protests in favor of democratic representation for elections are, however, casting a shadow over Hong Kong, or Fragrant Harbor, as it is also known. A call for democracy is the authentic enactment provided for in any legal election and electoral system free from 'unnecessary misunderstanding' and suspicion.

5.8 Europe and Beyond: No Translation, No War

History records examples of conflicts caused by treaties and ultimatums erroneously translated or intentionally misinterpreted. Bilateral or multilateral treaties of peace are subject to translation. In this sense, Louis Kelly in his history of translation and interpretation in the West (1979), stigmatized the interpreter's role, stating that war and peace are largely the result of the work of translators. There has been no peace and no war without them in the course of human history. The history of treaties and diplomacy relies essentially on the role of interpreters in world politics (Roland 1999; Baigorri-Jalòn 2014).

An indefinite and flexible interpretation can make a difference either in a positive or negative way. Interpretation and translation are, in this sense, embedded in the history of humanity, and in particular in the history of the western world. As already noted in previous sections, countless wars have been triggered by misunderstanding, be it intentional distortion, manipulation or accidental ambiguity.

The current global political need to present war in a more acceptable way has generated a linguistic change related to the use of specific words and their technical definitions. A very clear example of this is the fact that declarations of war no longer exist, nor does a traditional way of waging war. There are, on the other hand, an increasing number of actions such as peacekeeping, peace-operations, maintenance of peace, peace-building and terrorism prevention. The final document, whether it is a peace treaty or declaration of war, is the result of diplomatic work carried out behind closed doors, which often calls on international laws. It is the tip of the iceberg, emerging from the network of secret negotiations and diplomacy and always through the mediation of translators and interpreters acting for the respective diplomatic delegations. The history of the Nurnberg Trials is a case in point and marks the history of modern interpreting (Skinner and Carson 2008, pp. 14–21). As these are highly confidential reports, the details of the translational process and its subsequent alterations and adjustments remain undisclosed.

Apart from great divides in concepts and cultural systems and geopolitical partitions, there may also be international friction when it comes to interpreting minor parts of a resolution or political entity. The United States of America followed by the singular third person 'is' was an alteration to the plural 'are,' which was used prior to the civil war. It goes against grammar rules, yet assertion of meaning and unity surpasses grammar rules. Articles can trigger international disputes and rekindle dangerous tensions. Regarding the conflict in the 'occupied territories' and the Arab-Israeli question dating back to the 'Seven Days War,' in the UN Approved Resolution n. 42 (Nov. 1967), there was no article defining 'the' before the English term. Consequently, the dispute was over the absence of the article, which led to different interpretations: Arabia required Israel to withdraw from all 'the' occupied territories, while Israel agreed to withdraw from part of the occupied territories. Thus the opponents were caught in the quagmire of a 'conflict over the definite article.'

Declarations of war and the manifestos that followed had to be drafted out in all the languages of the colonized peoples of the great empires. Examples of conflicts and warfare abound in the Western world, and there are many instances of historical misunderstanding or deliberate manipulation in multilingual declarations and treaties. Biased treaties will inevitably trigger further vindications and claims to redress, usually regarding land rights, territories, boundaries and borderlands. Inevitably after a war, there are occupations or loss of national territories resulting in new maps and alteration of former geopolitical assets.

5.8.1 Germany and Austria: The Congress of Vienna

The Congress of Vienna (1814–1815) was essentially the result of translation and interpretation: the wording of the treaty, which put an end to the Napoleonic wars, otherwise known as the Continental wars in Britain, was the result of the astute and secret diplomacy of Austrian Chancellor Klemens von Metternich, who served the Hapsburg crown. He masterminded the drafting of the negotiations in the many different languages. He acted as a sort of supreme invisible coordinator for all representatives, English, French, Russian and German, (Mounin 1964, p. 168) through his secretary, who was the 'real' translator. Embarrassingly, his secretary had the double role of translator and secret agent for different European national states[19] and manipulated the translations for all the parties and governments present (i.e. France, Great Britain, Prussia, Austria). At the Vienna Congress he acted both as a translator and liaison interpreter, translating for Prussia against Britain and for France against Prussia and Russia. Moreover, he did not restrict his activity to translation but drafted and manipulated the speeches for the conflicting parties' different speakers. He would thus simultaneously prepare speeches for and against the same debated issues. He saw to it that atmosphere in Vienna was enjoyable by organizing parties, amusements and balls. The Congress approved his drafts and minutes till June 1815. It is worth noting that the Congress was not an institutionalized Congress, as it never met in plenary sessions and the discussions between the great powers occurred informally and sometimes privately. The drafts with the deliberations of the Congress were approved and sent over to Paris, where they became the new Treaty of Paris (November 1815). It was the first time in Western history that a Congress was convened to end a war and that national representatives came together to draft and formulate treaties, instead of relying on endless confusing dispatches and missives between the various courts of Europe, chanceries and ministries in the various capitals. The Congress actually shaped the face of international politics in Europe until the start of the First World War in 1914.

Another crisis ensued in northern Europe in July 1870, triggered by the claims to the Danish Duchy of Schleswig-Holstein, the crown of Denmark and Prussia. There was a deliberate misunderstanding, which paved the way for a state of political tension and ultimatum. The mastermind behind this was Otto von Bismarck, chancellor to Prussia and Kaiser Wilhelm I. The whole matter relied on a report of an encounter between Kaiser Wilhelm I and the French Ambassador. The dispatch or telegram was sent from Ems (Bad Ems), a thermal resort, to Bismarck. Bismarck manipulated and edited the version ensuring that it was published in a special newspaper supplement, with the aim of eliciting French outrage, thus paving the

---

[19] Metternich named his own aide, Friedrich Gentz, as secretary to the negotiations of Prussia, England, Russia, Austria plus France and Spain, whose representatives Talleyrand and Don Pedro Labrador, he tried to exclude from decisions and agreements. Sweden and Portugal were similarly incensed by their exclusion from the full Congress, especially since Metternich was determined to give the latter as little power as possible.

way for the Franco-Prussian war. Inevitably warfare in Europe was multilingual and there was constant multilingual translation of legal instruments. This occurred not only between states, but also at a national level.

5.8.2 First World War Manifesto

The languages of the Austro-Hungarian Empire, apart from Latin and German, were Hungarian, Czech, Croatian, Romanian, Slovak, Slovene, Dutch, Italian, Polish, Ruthenian, Bosnian and Serbian. When there were job calls for civil servants, even at a low rank, local dialects were required. The army of the Austro-Hungarian Empire had military instruction manuals in the languages of the Empire and the corps were selected according to the languages of the soldiers and their instructors, e.g. Croatian Grenzers (*Grenzen* → borders) Hungarian grenadiers, Houssars, Tyrolean Jaegers (Hunters of the Alps). Eleven peoples and nine official languages.

The declaration of war and call to conscription in 1914 were issued in all of these languages.

The summons was issued by Kaiser Franz Josef of Hapsburg in all the languages of the Empire, starting with the formula 'To all of my peoples.' It marked the outbreak of the First World War and it also reflected the multi-ethnicity of the empire. There was a notification of the 'beginning of a state of war to the Royal Serbian Government' and simultaneously the manifesto of the 'fateful hour' addressed to 'my beloved peoples' on July 1, 1914 beginning with the formula *An Meine Völker*, translated into English:

> To my people!
> It was my fervent wish to consecrate the years which, by the grace of God, still remain to me, to the works of peace and to protect my peoples from the heavy sacrifices and burdens of war. Providence, in its wisdom, has otherwise decreed. [...]
> With a quickly forgetful ingratitude, the Kingdom of Serbia, which from the first beginnings of its independence as a State until quite recently, had been supported and assisted by my ancestors, has for years trodden the path of open hostility to Austria-Hungary.

The opening preamble is a template, yet what follows is slightly different, as it targets different nations. The war was not bilateral, but involved many different nations. The Italian manifesto focuses on the Italian government, imputing the state of war to the King of Italy, 1 year later, on 23 May 1915:

> Il Re d'Italia mi ha dichiarato la Guerra. Una fellonia quale la storia non conosce eguale, venne perpetrata dal regno d'Italia verso i suoi due alleati. Dopo un'alleanza di più di trent'anni, durante la quale essa poté aumentare il proprio possesso territoriale e assorgere a insperata prosperità, l'Italia Ci abbandonò nell'ora del pericolo e passò a bandiere spiegate dai nemici.

> ENGLISH TRANSLATION

> The King of Italy has declared war on me.

Perfidy whose like history does not know was committed by the Kingdom of Italy against both allies. After an alliance of more than thirty years' duration, during which it was able to increase its territorial possessions and develop itself to an unthought-of flourishing condition, Italy abandoned us in our hour of danger and went over with flying colours into the camp of our enemies.[20]

This is the conclusive paragraph, hailing the glorious virtue of the troops. Trieste, Trentino, Friuli and the city of Gorizia (Goerz) were part of the Austrian Empire, where Italian was the language along with other local languages and German. The concluding ritual invocation to the Almighty 'to bless our banners' and thanksgiving to the troops:

Io saluto le mie truppe ferme nella lotta, abituate alla vittoria; confido in loro e nei loro duci. *Confido nei miei popoli*, al cui spirito di sacrificio senza pari vanno i Miei più sentiti ringraziamenti. All'Altissimo rivolgo la preghiera, che Egli benedica le Nostre bandiere e prenda la Nostra giusta causa sotto la Sua clemente custodia.

The English version below is available online. Compared to the Italian is has less emphasis, and imperial rhetoric is diluted. For example: '*ferme nella lotta* (steadfast in the struggle); 'I rely on them' is a reduction for 'I trust my peoples.' *Völker* ('peoples') with *Vaterland* is loaded with the power of allegiance as it is used in declarations that are lost in the English version. Furthermore the term 'rely' is a mild substitute for the Italian 'Confido'.[21] There are implications of faith and honor set in binary opposition to the Italian *felony*. There is a permutation in 'paternal' for 'sentiti' (heartfelt) and the 'Miei' (My) is not capitalized. 'That He may bless our banners' again loses in terms of reverence to the Almighty. 'Gracious protection' for 'clement custody' is more of a cliché.

I salute my battle-tried troops, who are inured to victory. I rely on them and their leaders. I rely on my people for whose unexampled spirit of sacrifice my most paternal thanks are due. I pray the Almighty to bless our colors and take under His gracious protection our just cause.[22]

---

[20] This anonymous English version was of course not part of the official documents, Italian and German here. With the anniversary of the First World War and memorial celebrations after 100 years, a massive number of primary documents in translation and in original languages are now available on dedicated websites . The English translation of the German and Italian declaration is anonymous. http://www.firstworldwar.com/source/italywardec_franzjosef.htm (Access October 10, 2014). Source: *Source Records of the Great War*, Vol. III, ed. Charles F. Horne. National Alumni. 1923.

[21] 'Confido' is the first word of the Catholic prayer 'Confiteor' and resonates with religious faith, and extends 'to trust' and 'entrust.' The German term for 'trust' is based on the word */true/* (faithful, loyal) and the German term *Trost* signifies 'comfort, relief.' The idea of 'trust' is substituted with the mildly managerial 'rely/reliable'.

[22] This online translation is slighty diluted in connotation, in respect to the Italian version derived from the original German.

Imperial Foreign Minister Graf (Count) Leopold von Berchtold was appointed to handle the matter neutrally with a network of allies. A ten-point ultimatum was presented to Emperor Franz Josef on 21 July. The Count altered the ultimatum and added clauses. He then presented it to the Serbians on 23 July, one month after the assassination of Archduke Franz Ferdinand in Sarajevo. The Serbians refused to grant permission to Austro-Hungarian authorities to investigate, as it would have been a severe violation of the country's constitution and Serbian sovereignty. This was the one point in the ultimatum that was not accepted. There was also manipulation in the declaration of war: Franz Jozef read that the Serbians had already attacked. The Emperor's signature was on the document. Count Berchtold erased the untrue reference to Serbian aggression. He also withheld the Serbian reply and did not notify Germany. When Kaiser Wilhelm in Berlin read the declaration he was unaware that the war was already in progress. The history of declarations, statements, communiqués, dispatches and manifestoes of the First World War is replete with accidental and intentional misunderstandings. Legal and diplomatic translation and interpretation was massive task. Metaphors were created to elicit emotional response, varying from irony to truculent curse. Metaphors and definitions have made history in international relations and diplomacy: from 'scrap of paper' to 'blank check' to the reaction of German Chancellor Theobald von Bethmann-Holloweg: 'Italy has now inscribed in the book of the world's history, in letters of blood which will never fade, her violation of faith.'

5.9 Conflict Areas: Geographic Boundaries

The history of the Western world is interspersed with fatal oversights, failed notifications, misinterpretations in the flow of communication and intentional manipulation (Baker 2006). The official declaration of war between Japan and the United States in December 1941 includes an intentional difference related to time zones. The Japanese attack at Pearl Harbor on December 8, 1941 was followed the next day by president's Roosevelt famous 'day of infamy' speech to the Houses informing them that 'a state of war exists' between the United States of America and the empire of Japan.

The beginning and the conclusion of the Second World War is interspersed with conflicting interpretations of international law and geopolitical configuration in terms of boundaries and territories, partitions of areas and divided cities. Translation and geographical definitions played a determinant role, albeit not one overtly perceivable by the people and communities involved.

Another long-debated issue regarded the 'London Memorandum of Understanding' (Memorandum d'Intesa) between Italy and former Yugoslavia (i.e. Marshal Tito), signed in 1954. This followed the former 'Free Territory of Trieste' (1948–1954). In 1947 the United Nations Security Council approved a Resolution (n. 16 Article 24 Charter) for the creation of a free state in Trieste and the region surrounding it.[23] What followed was the crucial definition of the sovereignty issue of Zone A (Italy) and Zone B (Yugoslavia) in international law. The Allied Military Government administered Zone A, which was divided into peacekeeping and law-enforcement sectors protected by a command of 5,000 Americans (TRUST: the Trieste United States Troops) and 5,000 British (BETFOR: British Element Trieste Force), each comprising a brigade-sized infantry force and complete support units (Signals, Engineers, Military Police, etc.).

In terms of language definitions, the terms 'zone' 'territory' and 'frontier' are not synonyms. The 'occupied territories' with the Palestinian and Israeli conflicts and the East Bank of Gaza are a case in point. The term 'zone' however, implies marking, division for jurisdictional purposes and specifically defines: 'an area subject to a particular political, military, or government function, use or jurisdiction: a demilitarized zone' (Collins 2000), implying that it would be an occupation zone also under military control.' The official version, signed in London on October 5th, 1954, was in English and was registered in the United States on April 25th, 1954. The nations involved were the United Kingdom and Northern Ireland, the United States, the Republic of Italy and the Republic of Yugoslavia. The terms were loaded with meanings and included 'boundaries adjustment,' 'demarcation' and 'preliminary demarcation' as set by the Morgan line.[24] The following comes in paragraph 2 and 3, after the preamble,. It does not refer to national borders but to boundaries:

> 2. As soon as this Memorandum of Understanding has been initialled and the *boundary adjustments* provided by it have been carried out, the Governments of the United Kingdom, the United States and Yugoslavia will terminate military government in Zones A and B of the Territory. The Governments of the United Kingdom and the United States will withdraw their military forces from *the area north of the new boundary* and will relinquish the administration of that area to the Italian Government. The Italian and Yugoslav

---

[23] 'A permanent statute codifying its provisions was to become recognized under international law upon the appointment of an international governor approved by the Quadripartite Powers. On September 15, 1947, the peace treaty between the United Nations and Italy was ratified, establishing the Free Territory of Trieste.' http://en.wikipedia.org/wiki/Free_Territory_of_Trieste (Access 23 October 2014).

[24] This is the Italian version: "Non appena il presente Memorandum d'intesa sarà stato parafato e le *rettifiche alla linea di demarcazione* da esso previste saranno state eseguite, i Governi del Regno Unito, degli Stati Uniti e di Jugoslavia porranno termine al Governo militare nelle Zone A e B del Territorio. I Governi del Regno Unito e degli Stati Uniti ritireranno le loro Forze Armate *dalla zona a nord della nuova linea di demarcazione* e cederanno l'Amministrazione di tale zona al Governo italiano. I Governi italiano e jugoslavo estenderanno immediatamente la loro Amministrazione civile sulla zona per la quale avranno la responsabilità http://www.triesteitaliana.it/memorandum.htm (Access 5 October 2014). With this 'linea di demarcazione' compounds and houses were severed and divided. It is not a paradox that someone had a lounge in Italy and the entrance in Yugoslavia.

> Governments will forthwith extend their civil administration over the area for which they will have responsibility.
> 3. The *boundary adjustments* referred to in para 2 will be carried out in accordance with the map at Annex 1. 8 A *preliminary demarcation* will be carried out by representatives of Allied Military Government and Yugoslav Military Government as soon as this Memorandum of Understanding has been initialled and in any event within three weeks from the date on initialling (emphasis added).[25]

The drafting of the bilingual edition of the Memorandum clearly shows a discrepancy in attribution of meaning. 'Military zone' is not a 'protected area.'

The Italian version has 'zona a nord della nuova linea di demarcazione' whereas the English uses the neutral term 'area north of the new boundary.' 'Linea di demarcazione' is not the same as 'boundary adjustment,' which can have a geographical connotation, whereas the Italian version implies a graphic and geometrical precision. There are different collocational meanings implied here, and there is a geographic definition that may collide with a military or legal interpretation and ascribed meaning in translation. The English draft was the mandatory reference. The definition of boundary in international law, from the *Oxford Dictionary of Law* (1983), is as follows:

> *Boundary*: An imaginary line that determines the territorial limits of a state. Such boundaries define the limitation of each state's effective jurisdiction. They are three-dimensional in that they include the airspace and subsoil of the state, the terra firma within the boundary, and the maritime domain of the state's international waters and territorial area.[26]

It is interesting to compare the definition of frontier and boundary in the context of the Federal expansion on the American Continent.

In 1975 the bilateral Treaty was signed at Osimo and ratified 2 years later, triggering outrage and indignation from the entire population of Trieste, on grounds of international law. The Treaty reportedly definitively stopped respective claims over the former Free Territory of Trieste by Italy and Yugoslavia, as the London Memorandum only disestablished the territory de facto, but not de jure. The 'infamous' Treaty of Osimo is now considered null and void as the former Republic of Yugoslavia no longer exists.

What is usually required is an interpretation of all interpretations, which in most countries and conflicts is 'the legal interpretation' or juridical hermeneutics. One

---

[25] http://freeterritorytrieste.com/TREATIES/UN541005MEMORANDUMLONDRA.pdf.

[26] See further on the context and definition of 'frontier' and 'boundary' in the context of the American Indian tribal territories and the Westward expansion, i.e., the Oregon Trail, the Black Hills of Dakota.

international legal dispute related to terms of sovereignty, as Italy had apparently never interpreted the treaty in terms of giving up to permanent military occupation in the 'zone'.[27]

References

Alcaraz E, Hughes B (2014) Legal Translation Explained. Routledge, London
Austin JL (1962) How to do things with words: the William James lectures delivered at Harvard University in 1955. Oxford University Press, Oxford
Backhouse E, Bland J (1941) Annals and memoirs of the Court of Peking. Houghton Mifflin, Boston
Baigorri-Jalòn J (2014) From Paris to Nuremberg: The birth of conference interpreting, Benjamins Translation Library. Benjamins, Amsterdam
Baker M (2006) Translation and Conflict. A Narrative Account. Routledge, London
Beke T (2014) Litigation communication. Springer, Berlin
Belmessous S (ed) (2011) Native claims. Indigenous law against empire, 1500–1920. Oxford University Press, Oxford
Belmessous S (ed) (2014) Empire by treaty: negotiating european expansion, 1600–1900. Oxford University Press, Oxford
Bennion F (2002) Statutory Interpretation: A Code. Butterworths, London
Bermann S, Wood M (eds) (2005) Nation, language, and the ethics of translation. Princeton University Press, Princeton
Bielsa E, Hughes C (eds) (2009) Globalization, political violence and translation. Palgrave Macmillan, Basingstoke
Camden W (1639) Rerum Anglicarum et Hibernicarum Annales Regnante Elisabetha. Ludwig Batavorum, London
Cao D (2004) Chinese Law: A Language Perspective. Ashgate, Farnham
Cao D (2007) Translating Law. Multilingual Matters, Clevedon
Carpi D, Ward I (eds) (2008) Literature and law. Textus. 21(3):361–372
Chan HC (2002) Bridging the gap between language and law: Translational issues in creating legal Chinese in Hong Kong. Babel 58:2 127-144
Collins English Dictionary (2000) Collins, Glasgow
Cooke M (1995) Understood by all concerned? Anglo/aboriginal legal translation. In: Morris M (ed) Translation and the law. Benjamins, Amsterdam, pp 37–63
Cunico S, Munday J (2007) Translation and ideology. Encounters and clashes. The Translator 13:2
Eades D (1992) Aboriginal english and the law. Queensland Law Society, Brisbane
Ford L, McCormack D (2005) The murrinh-patha legal glossary: translating legal concepts across cultures. ESP 2:58–75
Grice PH (1975) Logic and conversation. In: Cole P, Morgan JL (eds) Speech acts. Academic Press, New York, pp 41–58
Greenblatt S (1991) Marvelous Possessions. The Wonder of the New World. Oxford University Press, Oxford
Iannelli M (2006) Unequal treaties. Dissertation M.Sc. University for Foreigners, Perugia. Not published

[27] On June 2, 1993 a boat of Italian fishermen was attacked by the Montenegro-Serbian coast-guard off the Adriatic coast in international waters. One young victim, a fisherman, was from the small village of Grado, near Trieste.

Inghilleri M (2010) You don't make war without knowing why. The decision to interpret in Iraq. The Translator. Special Issue. In: Inghilleri M, Harding SA (eds) 16(2):176–196
Inghilleri M, Harding S (2010) Translation and violent conflict. The Translator. Special Issue 16:2
Karttunen F (1994) Between worlds. Interpreters, guides, and survivors. Rutgers University Press. New Brunswick
Katan D (1999) Translating cultures. An introduction for translators, interpreters and mediators. St. Jerome, Manchester
Kelly L (1979) The true interpreter. A history of translation theory and practice in the west. Basil Blackwell, Oxford
Kriewaldt MC (1960) The application of the criminal law to the aborigines of the northern territory. West Aust Law Rev 5:1–50
Law Drafting Division of the Department of Justice of Hong Kong (2001) Legislative drafting in Hong Kong: Crystallization in Definitive Form, 2nd edn, http://www.justice.gov.hk
Legrand P (2005) Issues in the translatability of the law. In: Bermann S, Wood M (eds) Nation, language, and the ethics of translation. Princeton University Press, Princeton, pp 30–50
Masiola Rosini R (1988) Questioni Traduttive. Campanotto, Udine
Masiola Rosini R (1997) Pianeti Proibiti. Descrizione Traduzione Intertesti. Guerra, Perugia
Menghesha Y (2008) Translation and cultural diversity, inaugural speech, FIT XVIII World Congress, 4–8 August. The Foreign Language Press, Shanghai
Mingxing Y (2012) The principles and tactics on diplomatic translation: A Chinese perspective. Babel 58(1):1–18
Mok O (1995) Accessibility of specialized lexicon as criterion for quality assessment of legal translations. Babel 41(4):193–208
Mounin G (1964) Teoria e storia della traduzione. Einaudi, Torino
Neate G (2003) Land, law and language: some issues in the resolution of indigenous land claims in Australia. Paper delivered to the conference of the Association of International Forensic Linguists, Sydney
Newmark P (1988) A textbook of translations. Prentice Hall, London
Pagden A (1987) Dispossessing the Barbarian: the language of Spanish thomism and the debate over property rights of the Indians. In: Pagden A (ed) The languages of political theory in early-modern Europe. Cambridge University Press, Cambridge, pp 81–92
Poon EW (2002) The pitfalls of linguistic equivalence: the challenge for legal translation. Target 14(1):75–106
Pratt L (1992) Imperial eyes. Travel writing and transculturation. Routledge, London
Roland R (1999) Interpreters as diplomats: a diplomatic history of the role of the interpreters in world politics. Ottawa University Press, Ottawa
Rose CM (1985) Possession as the origin of property. Univ Chicago Law Rev 51:73ff
Schaffer F (1998) Democracy in translation. Cornell University Press, Ithaca
Skinner W, Carson T (2008) Working conditions at the Nuremberg Trials. In: Bowen M, Bowen D (eds) Interpreting yesterday today and tomorrow. Benjamins, Amsterdam, pp 14–21
Todorov T (1974) The Conquest of America: The question of the Other. Harper and Rown, New York
Valdéon RA (2014) Translation and the Spanish Empire in the Americas. Benjamins, Amsterdam
Veitch S (1999) Moral conflict and legal reasoning. EALT Series 1. Hart Publishing, Oxford
Ward I (1995) Law literature: possibilities and perspectives. Cambridge University Press, Cambridge
Xie S (2010) An integrated study of Chinese and western translation theories under the reconstructive vision of faithfulness, expressiveness, Elegance. Intellectual Property Press, Beijing
Xu Y (2000) Characteristics and requirements for diplomatic translation. China Trans J 3–38
Yang M (2008) On political equivalence in translating diplomatic terms. J PLA. University of Foreign Languages, pp 90–94
Yang M (2012) The principles and tactics on diplomatic translation. Babel 58(1):1–17

Chapter 6
Manipulating Treaties

'As man disappears from sight, the land remains'
Maori Proverb

'Man's law changes with his understanding of man. Only the laws of the spirit remain always the same'
Crow Proverb

6.1 Intranational Treaties: Maori and New Zealand

All the treaties forced upon the native populations in North America and South America were the result of manipulations and misunderstandings, intentional or accidental. This arose with written statements and prospective agreements that would be read out aloud and then tentatively summed up by native interpreters, who most of the time weren't up to the challenge of the text and the complicated legal language, as seen in previous sections. The sacred Indian territories and native soil on the American Continent was lost as a result of the many incorrectly translated treaties, distortions and intentional legal loopholes. The history of Indian Wars and Indian confinement to reservations is a history of a people wronged through peace treaties and the government of Washington. The history of the possession of New Zealand Maori soil by the British Crown is another story of unequal treaties. One interesting case is the Treaty of Waitangi (1840) in New Zealand. Even in the pre-treaty phase there was a whole string of deliberate mistranslations and cultural misunderstandings, which resulted in vast areas of the land being sold by the natives, with purchase deeds drawn up in English (Fenton 2001, pp. 1–17). The New Zealand Colonization Company was formed for the purpose of investing venture capital in the purchase and re-sale of lands in New Zealand in order to promote emigration to that country. This, at least, was the official claim and institutional payoff. It was an investment scheme with the blessings of civilization, religion and education, where land was bought cheaply from natives by wealthy farmers and speculators who would then invest in financing the future emigration of a young labor force from England, relieving it from overpopulation and unemployment (Burns 1989). The interpreter for the transaction was Dicky Barrett,

R. Masiola and R. Tomei, *Law, Language and Translation*,
SpringerBriefs in Law, DOI 10.1007/978-3-319-14271-5_6

trader, whaler and interpreter (Caughey 1998). However, buying and selling were alien to Maori cultural concepts and patterns of community behavior (cf. Mutu 1992, pp. 57–103). Furthermore, the deeds were laden with legal jargon and concepts as foreign to the interpreter (and whaler) as they were to the Maori. The deeds were concluded and the representative of the New Zealand Company, Edward Wakefield, was ready to buy (and sell) new lands for the company. Wakefield was totally oblivious to the fact that the Colonial Governor of New South Wales, also responsible for New Zealand, had declared that any land sales were null and void. At the time, he was unaware that all 'private purchase' and investment had come to an end with the Treaty of Waitangi and that consequently the British Government had finally extended its rule of laws to New Zealand. What followed was an investigation into the legality of such deeds. William Spain, a lawyer, was appointed Land Commissioner of New Zealand by Lord John Russell, Colonial Secretary. This is a brief extract of the deeds that were examined as evidence of the scheme during court hearings. It was no longer a matter of tricking the natives, but of going against the rule of the Crown:

> Be it therefore known...have this day sold and parted with all our right, title and interest in all the said lands, tenements, woods, bays, harbours, rivers, streams and creeks, as shall be hereafter described...as a full and just payment for the same...to prevent any dispute and misunderstanding. And to guarantee more strongly ...the whole of the bay, harbour and district of the Wanga Nui Atera, commonly called Port Nicholson, situated on the north-eastern side of Cook's Strait in New Zealand (Caughey 1998: 104; in Fenton 2001: 14).

This is the verbatim back-translation Dicky Barrett provided to the court of his Maori version of the deed:

> Listen Natives, all the people of Port Nicholson, this is a paper respecting the purchasing of land of yours, this paper has the names of the places of Port Nicholson. Understand this is a good book. Listen the whole of you Natives – to write your names in this Book – and the names of the places – are Tararua continuing on to the other side of Port Nicholson to the name of Parangarahau ....(Ibid.)

The point is that the court wanted to see more clearly how the native chiefs had appended their signatures as they could not have understood anything of the legal language of a document of 1,600 words, which Barrett reduced to 115, and did not understand himself. Apparently Barrett had coaxed the chiefs into signing, explaining that their names might be seen by the Queen and that she would then know they were chiefs. This would give them a certain prestige, and they would possibly be sent gifts. The legality of the deed was questionable, but the reality was that British settlers had been caught in the scheme and had paid for the land. The outcome was a court ruling to the effect that the New Zealand Company had to pay compensation. Dick Barrett, together with his contemporary Henry Williams, the translator of the Treaty of Waitangi played a significant role in the country's takeover by the British, and yet neither of them was familiar with legal jargon, laws and the Maori language. Land claims going back to 1840 are still being heard in New Zealand's courts (Fenton 2001, pp. 16–17).

The Treaty of Waitangi was aimed at securing British sovereignty over New Zealand. It aimed at putting an end to decades of war with the Maori, but the result was that it engendered further rebellion and distrust. The first decades of the nineteenth century saw the outbreak of the 'Musket War' an inter-tribal war in which some twenty thousand Maoris were killed (1810, 1820, and 1830), using muskets brought over by Europeans. The 1840 Treaty of Waitangi aimed at ending inter-tribal warfare in order to protect the Maori, regulate British subjects and secure commercial interests. Wars between Maoris and Europeans over the possession of territories in the Waikato and Tarakai areas, however, continued from 1860 to 1863 (Orange 1987). The Waikato war started with the invasion by the British Army (July 1863). The most important battle was fought at Rangiriri. Even though Maori continued fighting for some 9 years, with this battle they had lost the war and lost their countries (November 1863). The events took place despite the Waitangi Treaty, signed 20 years before. The Treaty was prepared in a few days (February 1840), and a missionary man, Henry Williams, and his son translated the English draft into Maori overnight. The Maori chieftains (*Rangatiratanga*) were persuaded to sign with reassurances that they would retain authority. Many supported the agreement, and 540 signed the document which was sent around the country. There were some that refused, while others remained uncertain. The Colonial Office extended and enforced the Treaty to Maori tribes whose chiefs had not signed. The Treaty is not considered part of New Zealand domestic law, with the exception of principles referred to in Acts of New Zealand Parliament. The exclusive right to determine the meaning of the Treaty rests with the Waitangi Tribunal, a commission of inquiry created in 1975 to investigate alleged breaches of the Treaty by the Crown.[1] What follows is an English version of some of the articles of the Treaty and the back-translation by Sir Hugh Kawaharu from the 'original' Maori version by Henry Williams.

ENGLISH VERSION

Article the First

The Chiefs of the Confederation of the United Tribes of New Zealand and the separate and independent Chiefs who have not become members of the Confederation cede to Her Majesty the Queen of England *absolutely and without reservation all the rights and powers of Sovereignty* which the said Confederation or Individual Chiefs respectively exercise or possess, or may be supposed to exercise or to possess over their respective Territories as the *sole Sovereigns thereof.*

Article the Second

Her Majesty the Queen of England confirms and guarantees to the Chiefs and Tribes of New Zealand and to the respective families and individuals thereof the full exclusive and undisturbed possession of their Lands and Estates, Forests, Fisheries and other properties which they may collectively or

[1] Documents on old land claims are also available online at: http://www.justice.govt.nz/tribunals/waitangi-tribunal/documents/theme-research-reports/a-old-land-claims. Access 22 October 2014.

individually possess *so long as it is their wish and desire to* retain the same in their possession; but the Chiefs of the United Tribes and the individual Chiefs yield to Her Majesty the *exclusive right of Preemption* over such lands as the *proprietors thereof may be disposed to alienate* at such prices as may be agreed upon between the respective Proprietors and persons appointed by Her Majesty to treat with them in that behalf.

BACK-TRANSLATION FROM MAORI

The First

The Chiefs of the Confederation and *all the Chiefs who have not joined* that Confederation give *absolutely to the Queen of England forever the complete government* over their land.

The Second

The Queen of England agrees to protect the chiefs, the subtribes and all the people of New Zealand in the unqualified exercise of their chieftainship over their lands, villages and all their treasures. But on the other hand the Chiefs of the Confederation and all the Chiefs will *sell land to the Queen at a price agreed to by the person owning it and by the person buying* it (the latter being) appointed by the Queen as her purchase agent.

The above translation of the Maori text of the Treaty was done by former tribunal member Sir Hugh Kawharu, Maori leader and former university lecturer. In the Maori text of Article 1, the Maori gave the British a right of governance, *kawanatanga,* whereas in the English text, Maori ceded 'sovereignty'. One of the problems that faced the original translators of the English draft of the Treaty was that the British understanding of the word 'sovereignty' had no direct translation in the context of Maori society. *Rangatira* (chiefs) held the autonomy and authority, *rangatiratanga*, over their domains, but there was no supreme ruler of the whole country. In the Maori version, the translators used the inadequate term *kawanatanga*, a transliteration of the word 'governance', which is very different from 'sovereignty'. In Article 2, the Maori version uses the word *rangatiratanga* in promising to uphold the authority that tribes had always had over their lands, emphasizing status and authority. In the English text, the Queen guaranteed the Maori the undisturbed possession of their properties, including their lands, forests, and fisheries for as long as they wished to retain them, with an emphasis on property and ownership rights. The time reference 'forever' has been added in the Maori version. Needless to say, legal expertise is required to define and understand the right of 'preemption' in terms of British common law. The Oxford Dictionary of Law links it to 'option to purchase' and in updated versions records that:

> The right of first refusal to purchase land in the event that the grantor of the right should decide to sell. For example, if A makes a covenant that for 5 years he will not sell his land

other than to B at £ 5000, A cannot be forced to sell but B's right of pre-emption prevents him from selling to other than on the stated terms for 5 years. A right of pre-empion is valid only if it is sufficiently precise. A right of pre-emption created in registered land after 13 October 2003 is registrable as a restriction on the proprietorship register of the affected land.

The Maori believed they had ceded to the Queen a right of governance in return for the promise of protection, while retaining the authority they had always had to manage their own affairs. The facts, however, proved to be far from their belief and trust.[2] Land claims and legal actions totaled almost two thousand.[3] The Crown signed a Deed of Settlement with the Waikato-Tainui community in 1995. This included a formal apology for the actions taken in the wars of the 1860s and their legacy.

6.2 The Trail of Broken Treaties and North-American Indians

As seen in the first and second section of chap. 5, in colonization and expansion there is a recurrent manipulation of key concepts like possession, sovereignty, boundaries and territory in the sequel of manifestoes, agreements, and treaties. The history of the North American Indians is very similar to that of other colonies with the same problems related to culture, concepts, land and possessions (Prucha 1994). The metaphor of the 'Trail of Tears' for Indian deportation from native land has parallels with the 'Trail of Broken Treaties'. The number of broken treaties, however, is staggering: 500 treaties broken, nullified, and changed in the course of the infamous history of the reservation system, the Appropriation Acts (1871) and the Removal Act (1830), a law passed during the presidency of Andrew Jackson. This law authorized the president to 'negotiate' the removal of the major Indian tribes from their homeland in the southern states to federal territories west of the Mississippi river. It was a transplantation of the Indian Nation, supported by the whites, who were eager to access and exploit those lands. Tribes and families were subsequently deported from one territory to another and from one reservation to another. Unfair laws were passed, unequal treaties were signed, and most of them

[2] 2014 is the year of remembrance and war memorials. In 1945 together with the Anzacs, Maori were engaged in the liberation of the territories occupied by the German administration (Adriatisches Küstenland). The troops led by the New Zealander General Freyberg were the first to liberate Trieste, protecting the city from the incoming Titine Army (IX Korpus).

[3] "In 1995, New Zealand's Parliament heard how the invasion of the Waikato in 1863 was: wrongful and totally unjustified … the confiscations were unjust, and … Waikato-Tainui, far from being in rebellion, were in fact defending hearth and home … The Waikato war and the confiscations that followed caused devastation … The people were dispersed, and there was widespread suffering, distress and deprivation … The land of their ancestors had been taken from them with the stroke of a pen". http://www.nzhistory.net.nz/politics/treaty/the-treaty-in-practice/waikato-tainui. Access 23 October 2014.

were broken. Many tribes, moreover, did not benefit from these 'broken treaties' and never received recognition from the federal government. They thus remained outside the 'reservation trust-land' and federal programs.

Over time, some key terms related to space and geography became loaded with new meanings, particularly in the context of the colonial legal terms. The concept of boundaries, frontiers, prairies and plains, for example, as determined by the natural morphology of the American continent is recurrent in such treaties and has different denotations and significance (Carlson 1998; Hurt 2002). With the Westward Expansion, these terms have become key concepts in the history of language and geography, and in the history of colonization through treaties (Lazarus 1991; Nabokov 1999; West 2009; Zinn 2003). If there is a loss of connotative meaning in translating these terms into European languages, the semantic loss of 'legal' meaning is irreparable and irretrievable. It was impossible for the American Indians to understand all the legal implications, and as a result they lost their lands. The meaning of /boundary /here, for example, is totally different from that in the context of the London Memorandum previously analyzed.

The current definition of the term *boundary* is: 'something that indicates the farthest limit, as of area; border' (CED 2000). In British English, it coexists with the more literary form of */bourne, bourn/* (ca 1600; from the Old French *borne*).[4] The term */frontier* /often collocated with 'wild', features a new landscape and is currently defined as: 'the region of a country bordering on another or a line, barrier, etc., marking such a boundary' (CED 2000).

In the context of the American expansion to the west and the plains, the two terms overlap and define an extreme limit, the farthest limit. Boundaries, however, had to be set by government surveyors according to the needs of white settlers, pioneers, colonists, hunters and miners, and along the new railways. The case of the Mason-Dixon Line is significant for its metaphoric meaning of the cultural division of slavery and non-slavery states.[5] The original intent was to settle a demarcation dispute between the states of Pennsylvania and Maryland (1738).

The Wild West was the Wild Frontier. In American English, the term used for the Great Plains is the French word prairie (ca 1800; Old French from Latin *pratum* grass field, meadow). The following definition in the American legal dictionary (Osborn 2013 [1913]) is in stark contrast to the apportionment of land and the extortion of ancestral Indian territories:

---

[4] The term is more familiar as used in Shakespeare's *Hamlet* monologue.

[5] Charles Mason (astronomer) and Jeremiah Dixon (surveyor) set up the line in 1738. It was made up of blocks of limestone. It became widely known as the symbolic divider between the northern non-slave and the southern slave states during America's Civil War. The original Mason-Dixon Line was actually a *demarcation* (*or border*)*line* between Pennsylvania and Maryland, created in an effort to settle an 80-year land dispute between the two colonies. It also included the western border of present-day Delaware, as it was then a part of the Pennsylvania colony. See also http://www.worldatlas.com/webimage/countrys/namerica/usstates/lgcolor/mdmasondixon.htm. Access 23 September 2014 (emphasis added).

> An imaginary line, natural or artificial, marking the division of contiguous parcels of land. Boundaries are determined by acts of the owners, by statutes or orders or legal presumption. It is important to determine boundaries in many types of legal actions including the recovery of land, trespass and nuisance.

The concept of space is rich in symbolic national values clashing with the spiritual beliefs and cosmic harmony of 'heaven-and-earth' tribal and ancestral Indian narrative. It is often used with the concept of 'prairie', borrowed from the French *prairie* meaning 'open meadow'. New frontiers and territories, native resistance to massive encroachment on their land and environmental exploitation created a new vision of the American space and place as a cultural ideal (Brown 1970) on both sides. The conceptualization of space and place and subsequent narrative and representation take place within the framework of time. Regarding maps and descriptions of the territory in treaties, temporal signposts, deadlines and expiration were determinant in the application of the law. In this context, American-Indian interpreters were faced with an almost impossible task when they acted as mediators in treaties, negotiations and, eventually, reconciliation (Kawashima 1989; Karttunen 1994; Roland 1999).

The history of reconciliation, redress, compensation had one prophetic voice in Helen Hunt Jackson (1830–1885). In 1881 she highlighted the plight of native Americans to Congress, sending each member a copy of her *A Century of Dishonor* at her own expense: 'to redeem the name of the United States from the stain of a century of dishonour'. Helen Jackson's survey features the histories of seven different tribes, emphasizing aspects of justice and law following the disastrous effects of the 1871 'Indian Appropriations Act'. This work was not reprinted until 1964. The author also presented a bill aimed at creating Indian reservations and Indian schools, but it was rejected. The 1960s and 70s were the decades of Indian political movements and civil rights protests and saw the centenary anniversary of the treaties and the abolition of slavery.

One important episode in the civil rights movements at that time is the 'Trail of Broken Treaties Caravan' also known as the 'Pan-American Native Quest for Justice', when in November 1971 the American Indians Movement (AIM) took over the Bureau of Indian Affairs in Washington for several days. This came after President Richard Nixon had signed the 'Termination Act', another law detrimental to the American Indian nation. Under the 'Termination Act', former federal supervision and subsidies were to be administered by the individual states where the tribes had settled, leaving them virtually without social benefits. In 1924, Native Americans were granted citizenship, but they weren't granted voting rights until 1948 after their contribution to the Allied Forces victory. In the fifties (1954–1960), some sixty tribes suffered forced 'relocation', in compliance with a social program aimed at transforming them into either cheap land laborers or proletarian 'urban' dwellers. Ten years later in 1971, the American Indian Movement (AIM) organized the protest march known as the 'Trail of Broken Treaties Caravan'. This was a cross-country protest march (wagons, buses, trucks, etc.) to Washington, to present a '20-Point Position Paper' against President Nixon's Termination Act. The march was also a demonstration of support for the occupation of the 'little island of

Alcatraz', where Indians were shot by the FBI.[6] The following is the *Preamble to Trail of Broken Treaties with 20-Point Position Paper, significantly subtitled An Indian Manifesto. Restitution, Reparations, Restoration of Lands for a Reconstruction of an Indian Future in America.*[7]

> We need not give another recitation of past complaints nor engage in redundant dialogue of discontent. Our conditions and their cause for being should perhaps be best known by those who have written the record of America's action against Indian people. In 1832, Black Hawk correctly observed: You know the cause of our making war. It is known to all white men. They ought to be ashamed of it.
>
> The government of the United States knows the reason for our going to its capital city. Unfortunately, they don't know how to greet us. We go because America has been only too ready to express shame, and suffer none from the expression – while remaining wholly unwilling to change to allow life for Indian people.

There are some points that are particularly interesting from a legal perspective, such as the link with civil rights and constitutional, federal and state laws. The real challenge seems to be agreeing on new treaties after 500 broken ones in 200 years. Some of the 20 points listed below highlight the need to be exempted from state jurisdiction:

Restoration of Constitutional Treaty-Making Authority;
Establishment of Treaty Commission to Make New Treaties;
Commission to Review Treaty Commitments and Violations,
Resubmission of Unratified Treaties to the Senate;
All Indians to be Governed by Treaty Relations;
Mandatory Relief against Treaty Rights Violations;

---

[6] "…when AIM occupiers built fortifications and took up arms and munitions, both Wilson and the federal government (FBI, U.S. marshals, and BIA police) moved in. In the well-publicized 71-day occupation that followed, two AIM members were killed. Ultimately, AIM leaders negotiated a 'peace pact' with the government stipulating that the activists would be treated fairly and that the federal government would conduct a *fair review of several treaties.*

Although the immediate standoff was defused, tensions between Wilson's goon squad and AIM members continued over the next several years. Dozens of AIM members, including early founding members Russell Means and Dennis Banks, *were indicted on dozens of charges related to* the Wounded Knee standoff, but the charges were ultimately *dropped when a federal judge acknowledged spurious activity and involvement by the FBI* (emphasis added) http://www.aimovement.org/ggc/trailofbrokentreaties.html. Access 24 October 2014.

[7] The whole document is available posted by AIM: American Indian Movement founded in 1968. The episode of the occupation of Wounded Knee has negative comments, emphasizing the AIM violence, yet it is AIM members who were shot. The quote is from 'Legal Dictionary' http://legal-dictionary.thefreedictionary.com/Trail+of+Broken+Treaties. Access 25 October 2014.

Land Reform and Restoration of a 110-Million Acre Native Land Base
Revision of 25 U.S. Code §163 on the Role of Indians
Restoration of Rights to Indians Terminated by Enrolment and Revocation of Prohibition against 'Dual Benefits' of the Laws enacted under Public Law 280 (1953)
Resume Federal Protective Jurisdiction for Offenses against Indians
Creation of an 'Office of Federal Indian Relations and Community Reconstruction'
National referendums, Local Options and Forms of Indian Organization

What emerges here is the call for new treaties, federal laws and referendums empowering the Indian nation. The clearly articulated point on 'Judicial Recognition of Indian Right to Interpret Treaties' epitomizes the need for correct interpretation of the treaties as a legal right. The request is aimed at preventing manipulation and distortion in the interpretation of applicative measures and treaty enforcement.

> Judicial Recognition of Indian Right to Interpret Treaties:
>
> The Congress should by law provide for a new system of federal court jurisdiction and procedure, when Indian treaty or governmental rights are at issue, and when there are non-Indian parties involved in the controversy, whereby an Indian Tribe or Indian party may by motion advance the case from a federal District Court for hearing, and decision by the related U.S. Circuit Court of Appeals.[8] The law should provide that, once an Interpretation upon the matter has been rendered by either a federal district or circuit court an Indian Nation may, on its own behalf or on behalf of any of its members, if dissatisfied with the federal court ruling or regarding it in error respecting treaty or tribal rights, certify directly to the United States Supreme Court a 'Declaratory Judgment of Interpretation', regarding the contested rights and drawn at the direction or under the auspices of the affected Indian Nation, which that Court shall be mandated to receive with the contested decision for hearing and final judgment and resolution of the controversy - except and unless that any new treaties which might be contracted may provide for *some other impartial body for making ultimate and final interpretations of treaty provisions and their application. In addition, the law should provide that an Indian Nation, to protect its exercise of rights or the exercise of treaty or tribal rights by its members, or when engaging in new activities based upon sovereign or treaty rights, may issue an interim 'Declaratory Opinion on Interpretation of Rights', which shall be controlling upon the exercise of police powers or administrative authorities of that Indian Nation, the United States or any State(s),* unless or until successfully challenged or modified upon certification to and decision by the United States Supreme Court - and not withstanding any contrary U.S. Attorney General's opinion (s)...solicitor's opinion(s), or Attorney General's Opinion(s) of any of the States (emphasis added).

The episode itself and the 20 points don't appear to receive adequate reference in European history books, while the media has largely focused on minority

[8] Circuit courts date back to the origins of common law systems. Henry II instituted the custom of having judges ride around the countryside ("ride circuit") each year to hear cases, instead of having cases moved over to London. Circuit court defines the division of the country for judicial administration. The UK is divided into six circuits. The U.S. states have state courts called circuit courts. Most are trial courts of general original jurisdiction See also http://en.wikipedia.org/wiki/Circuit_court. Access 11 September 2014.

communities and migrant communities. Today, however, legal issues and question of land claims are shared via social forums and dedicated pages.[9]

Given the differences in cultural patterns, beliefs and community values, there are other factors that make the treaties between Washington and the Indians different than other colonial and postcolonial treaties. One such factor is the geographical magnitude of the territory subject to encroachment by diverse European powers and settlements. Another is related to historical events and the European wars exported to the American continent. Subsequent intranational conflicts include the American Revolution and Civil War. The hegemony of the ruling class and the occupation and dispossession of the native soil met with fierce resistance. The series of treaties (500) and negotiations and the wars and epic battles fought over the centuries testify to the feeling of having been duped by treaties (Kappler 1904). The American Indians' lasting resistance was possible thanks to their warfare tactics, mobility and the fact that they were able to master the white men's weapons and tools a superior way, e.g. using guns while riding horses. Confining them to reservations would have meant life imprisonment, if not a death sentence. The regulations of the reservation and the amendments are akin to genocidal policies. Chief Black Hawk sums up this feeling of impotence in his famous phrase: 'How smooth must be the language of the whites, when they can make right look like wrong, and wrong look like right'.[10]

One of the main problems in negotiations and treaties was that of defining space and areas, defined in terms of acres, which were very difficult for the Native Americans to understand. They had no concept of 'thousand', for example, and the Ponca Indians of the Central Plains (from Nebraska to Oklahoma) adopted the metaphor of 'one box', as the payment remitted after signing a treaty was contained in coins stored in a box. However, the issues and challenges differed in time and space over a span of more than 200 years, as perceptions and significance did not coincide. For example, the Council of the Plain Indians preceded the treaty, where smoking the pipe together was a traditional ritual, a pledge to truth and honor in the discussion to follow. Gifts served as a prelude to negotiations, and more gifts were given (bribery) upon closing the meeting. Gifts for the Indians were intended as a bond, whereas the Europeans used them as 'expectations' of acceptance of the 'right of occupancy'.

> To the Plains Indians the council – the coming together – remained the key; the treaty was less important. For the Federal Government and its representatives, the treaty signed at the end of the council meeting mattered above all else; the council served only as a preliminary to the written agreement (Carlson 1998: 137)

[9] This is from a blog posted in 2011: 'If I were a true Native American, I would use old maps to find out the exact spot my forefather's owned, and *bring a suit in district court. I would take it all the way to the Supreme Court* if I needed to, this land was clearly obtained by false premise'.

[10] See also the exhibition (2014–2018) at the Museum of American Indian, New York: *Nation to Nation: Treaties Between the United States and American Indian Nations* on the history and legacy of U.S.–American Indian diplomacy from the colonial period through the present.

The Treaty in 1854 forced the Omaha into ceding most of their lands to the United States and resulted in them being confined to a reservation. In 1877, with another treaty and 'gifts' the Ponca tribe moved south to another Indian territory in Oklahoma, although they had wanted to stay in Nebraska, even if that meant being in a reservation. The imprisonment of Ponca leaders who returned to Nebraska by the US army was questioned before court. It resulted in the landmark civil rights case (1872), which established the recognition of rights for American Indians under the constitution.

> To the Plains Indians the Council – the coming together remained the key; the treaty was less important. For the Federal Government and its representatives, the treaty signed at the end of the council meeting, mattered above all else; the council served only as a preliminary to the written agreement (Carlson 1998: 137)

The treaties were not just of the type 'one tribe one treaty' or 'one land one treaty': there were subsequent treaties with the tribes till all the vast areas had fallen into government hands. In many cases it was not 'tribes' but different Indian nations (Shown 2014).

Negotiations, however, were not so peaceful and in many cases ensued from genocidal policies and land extortion. The ambiguity in interpretation, breach of mutual trust and manipulation occurred when the leaders who had appended their names and signed the treaty were no longer alive or responsible. Many of the treaties are named after the battles (Fort Laramie, Wounded Knee) that led to their signing. There are treaties with the warring Indian Nations: Apache (1852), Cheyenne and Arapaho (1865), Kiowa, Comanche and Apache (1867). In these treaties, it is interesting to note the wording of the preamble and first article. This is the Fort Laramie Treaty with the Sioux Lakota (1868), which ended the Black Hills Dakota War, wherein parties pledge their honor. The parties to the treaty are William Sherman and other generals and 'different bands' of the Sioux Nation of Indians against 'bad men':

> From this day forward all war between the parties to this agreement shall forever cease. The government of the United States desires peace, and its honor is hereby pledged to keep it. The Indians desire peace, and they now pledge their honor to maintain it.
>
> If bad men among the whites, or among other people subject to the authority of the United States, shall commit any wrong upon the person or property of the Indians, the United States will, upon proof made to the agent, and forwarded to the Commissioner of Indian Affairs at Washington city, proceed at once to cause the offender to be arrested and punished according to the laws of the United States, and also reimburse the injured person for the loss sustained.[11]

[11] 'Lieutenant General William T. Sherman, General William S. Harney, General Alfred H. Terry, General O. O. Augur, J. B. Henderson, Nathaniel G. Taylor, John G. Sanborn, and Samuel F. Tappan, duly appointed commissioners on the part of the United States, and the different bands of

The Treaty of New York (August 7, 1790) with the Creek Indians (14 Articles) is an example of 'land cession for goods' the Indians considered 'valuable'. Here as elsewhere, the Indian kings, chiefs and warriors appended their signature with an X. This was the first treaty signed in New York, and not in a contested region, under President George Washington.[12] It was a 'Treaty of Peace and Friendship' made and concluded by the president of the United States of America:

> Article I: There shall be perpetual peace and friendship between all the citizens of the United States of America, and all the individuals, towns and tribes of the Upper, Middle and Lower Creeks and Semanolies (sic) composing the Creek nation of Indians.
> Article II: The undersigned Kings, Chiefs and Warriors, for themselves and all parts of the Creek Nation within the limits of the United States, do acknowledge themselves, and the said parts of the Creek nation, to be under the protection of the United States of America, and of no other sovereign whosoever; and they also stipulate that the said Creek Nation will not hold any treaty with an individual State, or with individuals of any State.

Article IV has a definition of boundaries with indications and regulations to have them ascertained it by a surveyor:

> And in order to preclude forever all disputes relatively to the head or source of the main south branch of the river Oconee, at the place where it shall be intersected by the line aforesaid, from the Currahee mountain, the same shall be ascertained by an able surveyor on the part of the United States, who shall be assisted by three old citizens of Georgia, who may be appointed by the Governor of the said state, and three old Creek chiefs, to be appointed by the

(Footnote 11 continued)
the Sioux Nation of Indians, by their chiefs and headmen, whose names are hereto subscribed, they being duly authorized to act in the premises'. Documentation is available and was consulted at Yale Law School, Lilian Goldman Law Library, and the Avalon Project on Law, History and Diplomacy. http://avalon.law.yale.edu/19th_century/nt001.asp. Access 9 September 2014.

[12] This is the Preamble: "*A Treaty of Peace and Friendship made and concluded between the President of the United States of America, on the Part and Behalf of the said States, and the undersigned Kings, Chiefs, and Warriors of the Creek Nation of Indians, or the Part and Behalf of the said Nation*".

THE parties being desirous of establishing permanent peace and friendship between the United States and the said Creek Nation, and the citizens and members thereof, and to remove the causes of war by ascertaining their limits, and making other necessary, just and friendly arrangements: The President of the United States, by Henry Knox, Secretary for the Department of War, whom he hath constituted with full powers for these purposes, by and with the advice and consent of the Senate of the United States, and the Creek Nation, by the undersigned Kings, Chiefs and Warriors, representing the said nation, have agreed to the following articles.

> said nation; and the said surveyor, citizens and chiefs shall assemble for this purpose, on the first day of October, one thousand one hundred and ninety-one, at the Rock Landing on the said rigor Oconee, and thence proceed to ascertain the said head or source of the main south branch of the said river, at the place where It shall be intersected by the line aforesaid, to be drawn from the Currahee mountain. And in order that the said boundary shall be rendered distinct and well known, it shall be marked by a line of felled trees at least twenty feet wide, and the trees chopped on each side from the said Currahee mountain, to the head or source of the said main south branch of the Oconee river, and thence down the margin of the said main south branch and river Oconee for the distance of twenty miles, or as much farther as may be necessary to mark distinctly the said boundary.

There is an intention of defining and determining borders and areas very clearly. What is even more explicitly stated, apart from measurements, is this ominous statement: '*in order to extinguish forever all claims of the Creek nation, or any part thereof, to any of the land...*'. Compensation is defined as 'certain valuable Indian goods now in the state of Georgia' to be delivered to the Creek nation.[13] Behind the trail of broken treaties lies the advocacy of Indian independence (De Loria Vine 1985).

6.3 Conflicting Interpretations: East Africa

Now, after discussing of British and American intra-national treaties with the native population, and subsequent loss of their land, the focus shifts to the scenario of international conflicts and persisting diplomatic tension. As noted, the French version of Article 1 of the Resolution of the UN Security Council (22 November 1967) specifically requests withdrawal of Israeli forces from '*les territoires occupés*', while the English versions 'stylistically' omits 'the', implicating a 'generic' reference to territories, in the sense that it would imply 'one part but not all'. The Treaty of Küçük Kaynarca (today Bulgaria) between Russia and the Ottoman Empire was drafted in Italian, and its Russian and Turkish translations were quite different. It was signed on July 21st 1774 by the envoys of Katherine the Great and the representative of Sultan Hambud Hamid. Through this treaty 'The Sublime Porte' promised permanent protection to the Christian religion and churches. Similarly, the treaty of friendship between Russia and the United Arab Republic has differences in the two versions. In international treaties, there may be ambiguous formulations so as to offer flexible interpretations. In this sense the

---

[13] http://avalon.law.yale.edu/19th_century/nt001.asp. Access 9 September 2014.

'intranational' treaties differ from the proper 'international treaties'. In the latter, the contracting parties are aware of and prepared to accept ambiguity, as they deem an agreement, albeit imperfect, to be better than no agreement. This was not the case when European powers set out to extend their colonial dominions in Africa.

What follows is a clear example of distortion in interpretation and translation in the scramble for East Africa. The infamous bilateral treaty of Wuchale of 1889 between Ethiopia and Italy highlights the importance of treaty translation with all its dramatic consequences.

The Wuchale Treaty or Wichale (in Italian 'Trattato di Uccialli') is, however, only one example in a long line of agreements, pacts, conventions for mutual assistance and more general diplomatic activity related to colonial expansion in Africa and involving several European powers. A similar relationship had been established between France and Tunisia less than 10 years before. The new scenario in terms of treaties and diplomacy is that the relationship is not between the hegemonic power and the native inhabitants; it is between other European powers, like France and Great Britain. Emperor Haile Selassie himself provides an interesting narrative of the facts of this treaty and all the other diplomatic misunderstandings that occurred prior to the fascist invasion. They are recorded in his *My Life and Ethiopia's Progress* (1976), translated into English from the Amharic.[14]

On 2nd May 1889 Emperor Menelik II, former King of Shewa, signed the Treaty in his new role of King of Kings. The Treaty seemed to offer good opportunities for Italy to expand her possession to the northern territories and to include Asmara (modern Eritrea) and the Tigray highlands, proclaiming a protectorate in exchange for a sum of money, muskets and cannons. In September, Menelik rejected the claim. In October, he sent a missive to the King of Italy, which denounced the difformity of the two versions. Three years later, in 1893, Menelik denounced the treaty.

The Italian version of Article XVII read as follows:'Sua Maestà il re dei re d' Etiopia *consente di servirsi* del governo di Sua Maestà il re d' Italia per *tutte le trattazioni d' affari che avesse con altre Potenze o Governi*'. Literally this means: "His Majesty, king of kings of Ethiopia, *consents to avail Himself* of the government of His Majesty the king of Italy for *all trade transactions that He may have* with other Powers or Governments".

The subjunctive verb is the puzzling issue and implies that His Majesty the King of Kings of Ethiopia is subject to and conditioned by Italy in his dealings and transactions. There are dangerous implications well beyond an external offer of intermediation and good office. This statement of 'consent' means that any future

[14] The late Edward Ullendorff was an eminent British Ethiopianist. The introduction to the volume has interesting notes on the problems of finding English equivalents for Amharic, and the related cases of polysemy and ambiguity in the language of the law and diplomacy. He insisted in editing an annotated text although the Emperor at first seemed contrary to this idea.

activity regarding commerce and trade with other (European) powers must carried out through Italy. This clearly denotes cogency and deontic modality.[15]

The King of Italy, Umberto I expressed his deep disappointment when Emperor Menelik sent a letter (October 1890) to inform him that the text of the Italian version did not correspond to the Amharic version. The difference was that in the Italian version, Abyssinia consents or agrees to pass through Italy. The Amharic version had Abyssinia 'can' in the sense of option and choice, and not as a mandatory statement. The question caused endless debate and parliamentary discussion and ended in government crisis.

What is even more puzzling is how Menelik was made aware of the difference in translation. The history of this treaty curiously intertwines with other treaties, alliances, conventions and pacts, and the translational divergence came up amid the intricacies of diplomacy and networks with European governments. It so happened that 3 months before (July 1890), Menelik had invited the sovereigns of the Russian and British empires to his coronation. He was surprised to be informed that the aforesaid monarchs could not respond directly to him, by virtue of the treaty and in conformity with the general Agreement of the Conference of Berlin (1884), as Ethiopia's sovereignty was limited by the Italian protectorate.[16] It was like a 'treaty within a treaty'. The matter created tensions within the Italian government, mainly voiced by Francesco Crispi. He forcefully contested the Ethiopian interpretation of the treaty, leading to endless discussions. The different translation and interpretation of the verb triggered the *casus belli.* Crispi entrusted Count Pietro Antonelli to express his strong remonstrations. Count Antonelli more diplomatically sought to reach an agreement with Menelik on the delimitation of the borders between Ethiopia and the Italian colony in Eritrea. Menelik rejected his proposal and asked for a revision of the treaty before its expiration. Subsequently the relations between the two parties became very tense, culminating in the First Italo-Abyssinian War.[17] The Italian forces were ultimately defeated by Menelik's troops at the Battle of Adwa (March 1, 1896). The new Treaty of Addis Ababa (October 26, 1896) restored the southern part of the country to Ethiopia and acknowledged its absolute independence.

There is no doubt that there was an intentional mistake in translating the treaty to Emperor Menelik II, who appended his signature in good faith and who would

[15] The English reference online give an English translation which is syntactically different: "The Treaty of Wuchale stated that the emperor of Ethiopia 'could' have recourse to the good offices of the Italian government in his dealings with other foreign powers; but the Italian text of the treaty had the word 'must'". The problem is equating an Italian subjunctive with English deontics ('must'). http://www.britannica.com/EBchecked/topic/643083/Treaty-of-Wichale. Access 30 October 2014.

[16] The Italian Wikipedia depicts the treaty as a 'hoax': 'La truffa di Uccialli'. http://it.wikipedia.org/wiki/Guerra_di_Abissinia#La_truffa_di_Uccialli. Access 30 October 2014.

[17] Ethiopia started to import ammunitions with the money obtained from Italy as compensation for the Treaty. The main suppliers were the Russians, the only European nation who had openly sided with Ethiopia, and France, because of the deterioration with Italy following the Tunisia question. Oddly enough, the Italians sold weapons to Ethiopia.

never have accepted submission to a protectorate. In fact according to the Italian version, Ethiopia was obliged to conduct all foreign affairs through the Italian authorities, thus making Ethiopia an Italian protectorate, while the Amharic version simply gave Ethiopia the option of communicating with third powers, the international community, through the Italian government. The hidden work of translators, drafters and diplomats seems to blur boundaries here, as the parties to the treaty are required to sign the two versions. There is no need to point out how, in the case of oral traditions with no written translation and remote cultures and languages, it was quite easy to have blurred and fuzzy meanings, either intentional or accidental. Whatever the intention, such interpretative divergence often caused friction and conflicts.

In his autobiography (1892–1937) Emperor Haile Selassie narrates in detail a similar conflicting interpretative issue caused by manipulation or inexact correspondence in the versions of a convention. The matter is still contentious today as it deals with water resources and the Lake Tana reservoir. Some 10 years after Wuchale, a convention was signed by Menelik in 1902 and the British Government referred as …the convention for mutual assistance between the British Government, as regards the barrage at Lake Tana, and the Italian Government, as regards the construction of a railway from the border of Eritrea, cutting through the middle of Ethiopia, to Italian Somaliland'. The convention was also part of an agreement between the British and Menelik to send engineers to help the construction of the barrage, and the Ethiopian Emperor notes that:

> Subsequently, after the Great War (1919), the Italian Government despatched envoys to London and presented a proposal for mutual assistance in connexion with the British Government's Lake Tana dam and the Italian Government's construction of a railway from the border of Eritrea and cutting through the centre of Ethiopia. But as the British Government had begun to negotiate direct with the Ethiopian Government, the proposals which the Italian Government had presented to it remained for the time unacceptable. (125)

Italy pursued her aim of the construction of a motor-road or railway. So in November (1919) Italian envoys were in London to receive support from the British government, and presented the matter in the following terms. It is interesting to note the reference to further treaties, provisions of the agreements and the former 'Tripartite agreement', i.e., the Anglo-Franco-Italian accord (1906). The diplomacy of envoys, missives and agreements between Britain and Italy concerning a water supply in East Africa in 1925 was seen in terms of 'fiduciary responsibility for Egypt and Sudan and mindful in this respect of the value to Egypt'. Crucial terms include 'reservation' and other lexical items related to limits and boundaries, which are blurred in the Amharic version.

The Italian government, however, tried to bypass the Ethiopian government and directly set the agenda with Britain and Benito Mussolini. In the correspondence and the respective translations there are interesting notations on key legal terms defining boundaries, and diplomatic buzz-words, like *status quo* in Amharic rendered by descriptive periphrasis: 'so that Ethiopia should remain as she was'. There were flurries of accords and treaties, and the tripartite agreement was preceded by letters and discussions involving diplomatic envoys from the three or four nations. Referring to the events of 1919, Hailé Selassie's autobiography thus reports the question of British Somaliland and the building of a railway from the border of Eritrea cutting through the middle of Ethiopia up to Italian Somaliland:

> ...as a result the Italian Government negotiated and agreed with the British Government, at Rome, that the proposal which it had initiated in 1912 (=1919) be implemented; and exchange of correspondence ensued which embodied the text of the agreement. The two governments arranged for the text of the agreement, though allegedly only an exchange of correspondence, to be registered with the League of Nations at Geneva. While they did this, they did not inform, even by a single word, the sovereign Ethiopian Government. The following is the text of the letters of agreement which were exchanged (Haile Selassie 1976: 126).

The evidence is supported by the letters of agreement exchanged between Mussolini and the British Ambassador to Italy, Sir Ronald Graham.[18] This is from Sir Graham on 20th December 1925:

> When the British Government, mindful of the great value of the waters of Lake Tana, requests a concession from the Ethiopian Government for the construction of a barrage at Lake Tana, in the part given over to *Italian interests*, the Italian Government will support Great Britain. This is pending the delimitation of the *zone* given over to British interests and pending a full investigation of the *reservation* which Italy requires under the terms of the *Tripartite Agreement* (in Haile Selassie 1976: 127; emphasis added).

The English version cited above is an Amharic translation on which Ullendorff had to work. So the letters in English are a re-translation into English from the English-Amharic. Ullendorff carefully notes that the 'Amharic translation of these letters is neither very literal nor always very accurate' (Ullendorff nn. 11–16, in Haile Selassie 1976 : 127; nn. 11–16).

- The original letter had 'within the Italian sphere of influence', which is concentrated into a pragmatic 'Italian interests'. Ullendorff notes that it cannot refer to the physical 'Lake Tana region' but that it must be a reference to Italy's 'possessing a predominating interest in the area of Ethiopia'.
- 'The term reservation in this context almost certainly bears the connotation of a reserved tract of land'. So it is not intended as 'reservoir' or 'barrage' and has a different meaning compared to the Indian Reservation. The key terms here are also 'region', 'area' and 'zone'. The Tripartite Agreement was the Anglo-Franco-Italian accord of 1906.[19]

---

[18] Sir Joseph Austen Chamberlain (1924–1929), father of the more famous Neville was the Foreign Secretary. He was awarded the Nobel peace prize for the negotiation of the Locarno Pact (1925), which was actually made up of various treaties between European nations concerning the settlement of disputes by arbitration and the maintenance of frontiers. Germany violated the pact in 1936 with the occupation of Rhineland.

[19] The three governments pledged themselves to maintain the status quo in Ethiopia. Britain had a predominate interest in Lake Tana and the Blue Nile, Italy had an interest in connecting the colonies of Eritrea and Somalia, the French had an interest in the hinterland of the French Somali Coast. The Treaty aimed at preventing changes in the political conditions. Governments were pledged to consult each other if there were alterations.

The translation and notes quoted here are Edward Ullendorff's. He also had access to Italian authors, notably Luca dei Sabelli. There are still more discrepancies in the letter from the British Ambassador:

> When the British government asks the Ethiopian Government for a concession to construct a motor road from Lake Tana to Sudan, *it may request the Italian government to* support it. *This railway*, according to the Tripartite Agreement, *will pass to the west (sic) of* Addis Ababa. All the works necessary for the construction of this railway shall have a free passage across the above-mentioned motor road (Haile Selassie 1976: 127; emphasis added).

Again in the footnotes, Ullendorff meticulously observes:

- In the first sentence: 'The tenor of the original is somewhat different and refers to an Italian offer of such support'.
- In the second part a whole sentence has been omitted in the Amharic translation, and the English original read: 'Italy requests the support of Great Britain in order that she may obtain from the Ethiopian Government the concession to construct and to run a railway from the frontier of Eritrea to the frontier of Italian Somaliland'.
- 'This shows the vast extent of the projected Italian sphere of influence. If the words 'west of Addis Ababa' did not clearly appear in Article 4 of the 1906 Agreement, one might have thought that this was a simple error for 'east'. Luca dei Sabelli's comment (IV, 101) that this amounted in effect to a partition of Ethiopia is scarcely exaggerated.'

As in the case of the Memorandum of London and other treaties, defining precisely geographical boundaries and their equivalents in adequate translations of a treaty is as vital as correctly and adequately translating conditionals, modals and deontics (may, shall, must, etc.), which are not totally symmetrical in their performative force in different languages. Ullendorff tracks still more incongruities, similar to those in the Wuchale Treaty. These are more passages from the letter:

> Italy requests Britain to support with the Ethiopian Government all requests which she may submit for exclusive economic rights in the west of Ethiopia and in the territory through which the aforementioned railway will pass and for obtaining economic concessions in the *Italian zone.* She reserves the right to present the identical request to France (Ibid., emphasis added).

Ullendorff comments that 'no such zone had ever been requested, defined or granted'. There are yet more mix-ups here:

> Consequently, H.B.M's Government would welcome the offer of support made by Italy, provided there remain unaffected waters in which Egypt and the Sudan have such an interest and which the *Ethiopian Government* has long recognized (Ibid., emphasis added).

Possibly because of hastiness, the English version reads 'Italian' and not 'Ethiopian'. 'It is odd how the Ethiopian translator could have misread the unequivocal original text' is Ullendorff's apt comment in his notation of words in the Amharic alphabet. The analysis of Mussolini's letter is equally meticulous in which when he compares the Amharic, English and Italian and notes that 'the

Amharic translator did not always adhere closely to the original text' and detects omissions, false friends, erroneous interpretations and loss of connotation (p. 131 n. 22–29). For example the Italian term *esclusività* is a legal term, which is employed in private contracts for sole agents, 'agenti in esclusiva', and is not the generic 'special economic influence'. A similar term in Italian is *concessionario* and *concessione* signifying/agent/, as in commercial agent or sole trader, whereas the Amharic term suggest that the translator is thinking of economically advantageous prices.

Stylistically, Mussolini's letter is laden with extraordinary repetitiveness. In light of the gathering clouds of war, Mussolini's insistence on 'an undertaking by Italy not to construct any obstacles by the sources of the White Nile', which were wholly outside Italian control is rather odd (p. 134, n. 33). Subsequent to the aforementioned events, Emperor Selassie discussed the matter of the Lake Tana Dam scheme in London in 1924. Two years later (19th June 1926), he presented an appeal to the Secretary General of the League of Nations, Joseph Avenol:

> It did not seem to us proper to allow some members of the League of Nations to conclude an agreement among themselves and to force another member to accept their plan, *even if* it did not affect the national interests of that member (Ibid. 110; emphasis added)

According to Ullendorff the official translation of the 'even' clause is 'neither accurate nor logical' (Ibid. 110, n. 36). There are several diplomatic documents reported and cited in this autobiography in which diplomatic and legal translation is a crucial and sensitive issue. As Edward Ullendorff had a command of all the languages cited in the documents and treaties and had agreed with the Emperor himself to the use of footnotes. Therefore, manipulation, omissions and misinterpretations add to the evidence for a variety and typology of different inadequacies in translation. The accumulation of small oversights, underrating and a failure to grasp connotative meanings can thus create an atmosphere of reciprocal distrust. The mistakes are both syntactic and semantic, ranging from verbs to prepositions. The term 'concessione' in diplomatic protocol (see the French verb *octroyer*) implies that something is granted,[20] in 'concession' in the sense of 'lease'.

By way of conclusion, there seems to be a trend in legal terminology towards differentiating between a context-specific subject-oriented use of a term and a 'common' or standard use. Itemized definitions and contextualized entries are essential for verifying terminology and lexicon. (Sager 1990). The different meanings of a given legal term in the different branches of the law and different legal systems further complicate its interpretation, multilingual translation and culture-specific communication (cf. Temmerman and Van Campenhoudt 2014).

---

[20] The Italian *concessione di un diritto* corresponds to the English 'enfranchisement'. The phrasal verb used is *dare in concessione*.

6.4 Concluding Remarks

There are many examples of manipulation, and history abounds with intentional mistakes, misunderstanding, different interpretations and ambiguities. Furthermore, translation is a human activity and so it represents, in international contexts a commitment or a lack of commitment to openness and transparency in international relations on the part of national governments.

Now, the real challenge is to overcome linguistic barriers, in order to reduce and minimize errors, misunderstandings and blurred meanings in international communications, international legislation, negotiations and diplomacy. The importance of press releases and news coverage of events related to international law, civil rights, criminal law and extradition are paramount in the context of influencing public opinion and creating consensus. If objective information is for some almost impossible, if not 'bullshit', ethics in translation concerning legal matters may be attained by means of strategies and professional skills.[21]

Distortions and manipulations do occur, and the history of international relations and colonialism has numerous examples of agreements for which conflicting interpretations have triggered conflicts. These may have been intentional mistakes, misunderstandings, different interpretations or inadvertent ambiguities. Translation has an impact on the processes of globalization and internationalization. Preserving the linguistic rights of a community in terms of laws and policy issues, in contexts where identity is at stake (Cronin 2006) and linguistic 'diversity' seems to be declining, should be a priority; in this regard: 'Minority languages can be seen as the quintessential and emblematic expression of the local in the era of globalization' (Cronin 2003, p. 164). Furthermore, the 'quest for clarity' can still provide guidance (Paciullo 2014, pp. 15–19).

Errors may also come in a more subtle, less obvious form, such as an adverb, article or a punctuation mark that changes the perceived meaning of a sentence or a clause. They may also come in the form of polysemy and lack of lexical and conceptual symmetry, as seen in Chaps. 2 and 3. The importance of how the media reports on criminal cases in different languages (different Englishes) and the localization of crimes such as 'cattle stealing' is thematically analyzed in Chap. 4 along with the problems of globalization of crimes and violence. The implications of colonialism and postcolonial debate impacting on the global issues of today like civil rights, human rights (Garre 1999) famine and diasporic migration call for ethics in translation and competent communication—both of which are desirable and possible.

The common theme of all the chapters is the manipulation of language and the law to gain power (Conley and O'Barr 1998) and the translation of treaties in

---

[21] This was a hotly debated issue at the *International Festival of Journalism*, Perugia, 2014 at the presence of Om Malik.

colonial and postcolonial contexts. Investigating diasporic globalization and the law will require further systematic analysis of the salient dynamics that are shaping a new ethnography of legal discourse (Conley and O'Barr 1990) and its constitutional translatability in the new age of terrorism and mass migration. The situation is getting worse and its full extent is still unknown.

References

Brown D (1970) Bury my heart at wounded knee: an Indian history of the American West. Holt, Rinehart and Winston, New York

Burns P (1989) Fatal success. The history of the New Zealand Company. Heinemann Reed, Auckland

Carlson P (1998) The plains Indians. Texas University Press, Austin

Caughey A (1998) The interpreter. A biography of Richard 'Dicky' Barrett. David Bateman, Auckland

Collins English Dictionary (2000) Collins, Glasgow

Conley JM, O'Barr WM (1990) Rules versus relationship. The ethnography of legal discourse. University of Chicago Press, Chicago

Conley JM, O'Barr WM (1998) Just words. Law language and power. University of Chicago Press, Chicago

Cronin M (2003) Translation and globalization. Routledge, London

Cronin M (2006) Translation and identity. Routledge, London

De Loria V Jr (1985) Behind the trail of broken treaties: an Indian declaration of independence. University of Texas Press, Austin

Fenton S (2001) Possess yourselves of the soil: interpreting in early New Zealand. Translator 7(1):1–18

Garre M (1999) Human rights in translation. Legal concepts in different languages. Copenhagen Business School Press, Copenhagen

Hurt D (2002) The Indian frontier: 1763–1846. University of New Mexico Press, Albuquerque

Kappler C (1904) Indian affairs, laws and treaties, vol 2. Bureau of American Indian Affairs, Washington

Karttunen F (1994) Between worlds. Interpreters, guides, and survivors. Rutgers University Press. New Brunswick

Kawashima Y (1989) Forest diplomats: the role of interpreters in Indian-white relations on the early American frontier. University of Nebraska Press, Lincoln

Lazarus E (1991) BlackHills/white justice: the Sioux Nation versus the United States 1775 to the present. HarperCollins, New York

Mutu M (1992) Cultural misunderstanding or deliberate mistranslation? Deeds in Maori of pre-treaty land transactions in Muriwhenua and their English translation. Te Reo 35:57–103

Nabokov P (1999) Native American testimony: a chronicle of Indian-white relations from prophecy to the present. 1492–2000. Penguin Group, New York

Orange C (1987) The treaty of Waitangi. Allen & Unwin, Wellington

Paciullo G (2014) Globalization and private law. Tangram, Trento

Prucha FP (1994) American Indian treaties: the history of a political anomaly. University of California Press, California

Roland R (1999) Interpreters as diplomats: a diplomatic history of the role of the interpreters in world politics. Ottawa University Press, Ottawa

Sager JC (1990) A practical course in terminology processing. Benjamins, Amsterdam

Selassie IH (1976) My life and Ethiopia's progress. School of Oriental and African Studies, London
Shown HS (ed) (2014) Nation to nation. Treaties between the United States and the American Indian nation. Foreword Kevin Gover. The National Museum of the American Indian, New York
Temmerman and Van Campenhoudt (eds) (2014) Dynamics and Terminology: An interdisciplinary perspective on monolingual and multilingual culture-bound communication. Benjamins, Amsterdam
West E (2009) The last Indian war: the Nez-Percé story. Oxford University Press, New York
Zinn H (2003) A people's history of the United States: 1492-present. Harper Collins, New York

MIX
Papier aus verantwortungsvollen Quellen
Paper from responsible sources
FSC® C105338

If you have any concerns about our products,
you can contact us on
ProductSafety@springernature.com

In case Publisher is established outside the EU,
the EU authorized representative is:
Springer Nature Customer Service Center GmbH
Europaplatz 3, 69115 Heidelberg, Germany

Printed by Libri Plureos GmbH
in Hamburg, Germany